MONEYology

TURN YOUR WEALTH AROUND & ACHIEVE FINANCIAL FREEDOM

JO OUTRAM

Moneyology: Turn Your Wealth Around & Achieve Financial Freedom

© Joanne Outram 2021

www.jooutram.com

First published in England 2021 by Jo Outram

ISBN 978-0-6450673-5-4

Disclaimer

All the information, techniques, skills and concepts contained within this publication are of the nature of general comment only and are not in any way recommended as individual advice. The intent is to offer a variety of information to provide a wider range of choices now and in the future, recognising that we all have widely diverse circumstances and viewpoints. Should any reader choose to make use of the information herein, this is their decision, and the author and publisher/s do not assume any responsibilities whatsoever under any conditions or circumstances. The author does not take responsibility for the business, financial, personal or other success, results or fulfilment upon the readers' decision to use this information. It is recommended that the reader obtain their own independent advice.

Dedicated to...

*M*y niece, Paige.

My inspiration for writing this book, so that the next generation of women entrepreneurs have a healthier and wealthier life, from the very start of their career.

Foreword

Wealth, health and happiness.

These are the three things that most people want more of in life.

And, to a certain extent there are tried and tested ways to make them happen.

Earn more, spend less, invest wisely.

Eat healthy food, exercise more, breathe deeply.

Find what makes you happy and do more of that, more often.

These simple formulas work – sort of. But they're missing a key, essential ingredient.

Mindset.

And I'm not talking about affirmations or positive thinking or creating vision boards.

I'm talking about the combination of your thoughts, emotions, beliefs, values, habits, behaviours, strategies and history that when blended together create the outcome that is your life. Right now. As you know it.

Consider this.

All of your conscious and unconscious choices to date have led you here, to this moment, reading the forward of this book, which, when you apply the techniques you'll learn inside, will change your life.

Something about Moneyology attracted your attention. Perhaps by chance, but more likely by design.

And the choice is yours:

1. to read through it, thinking 'ooh, that's a good idea' or 'yes, I'll try that' and not taking action (kind of like picking up a recipe book, salivating at the picture of a plate of brownies yet not actually taking out the equipment and the ingredients and making them)

2. to read through it, thinking 'ooh that' a good idea' or 'yes, I'll try that' and then actually doing the activities that Jo, as the expert she is, recommends.

Because when you take action, however small, you shift the way you think, the way you feel, the way you behave and, of course, the results that you get.

When you become aware of your mindset and the way in which your thoughts, habits, emotions, beliefs and values influence your health, wealth and happiness, you are able to take control.

And to make things happen by design rather than default.

As the Founder of the Mindset Coach Academy, I train coaches like Jo in a comprehensive suite of neuroscience-based modalities that create change at the conscious and unconscious level.

As an MCA Alumni and Faculty Member of the Mindset Coach Certification program, Jo brings an easy to implement blend of money mindset and practical money know how to the wealth creation table.

Moneyology is not only a highly enjoyable read.

It's packed with a wealth of ideas and actions you can take to change your money story and become the custodian of your finances.

Jo has created a unique blend of practical money strategies, mindset shifting practices and straight- talking wake up calls designed to change the way you think, feel and act towards money.

Like that friend who is able to tell us "yes, your bum DOES look big in that" and still be our bestie, Jo has a way of engaging and compelling you to face your financial reality so that you can change your financial future.

This book isn't about sitting down and manifesting abundance – although it does equip you with Law of Attraction principles to more easily magnetise money to you.

This book isn't some dry tome full of financial formulas and spreadsheets that make you want to bury your head even deeper in the sand – it's a hold your hand guidebook that inspires you to pay attention to your money in the same way you would a new baby, an exciting new lover or that block of Lindt chocolate you love.

This book isn't full of actions that sound good on paper but don't actually work in reality.

Moneyology is the ultimate guide to creating the money mindset and money know how you need to create the abundance you desire.

Enjoy,

Lara Young
Founder and Master Coach Trainer
The Mindset Coach Academy

Table of Contents

"It's never too late – never too late to start over, never too late to be happy."

JANE FONDA

Introduction

*I*t's a common dream to become wealthy, to have enough money, so that you never have to worry about paying the bills; so that you can hop on a plane and jet off to your ideal holiday destination; so that you can have the house of your dreams and support the causes and charities close to your heart.

Here's where it gets exciting, because you can turn this dream into reality. Ignore negative Nelly in the back of your mind saying "not you"; you'll soon learn that she isn't the fount of all knowledge, and that while she has the best of intentions her knowledge base is flawed.

Here's the sting in the tail though – you will have to make some changes to make this happen. Let's face it, your current mindset about money and wealth has resulted in the financial position you are currently in. If you are where you want to be then that's great, but if you aren't near to your dream of what a wealthy life looks like, then you'll need to make changes.

Just take some time to think about this – your current mindset about money has created your current circumstances. It's not been the economy or anyone else, it's been your beliefs. If you aren't ready to take responsibility for the significant role you've played in your financial situation to date, then put this book down. Seriously, if you aren't ready to jump into the driver's seat then you aren't going to make the changes necessary.

The good news is that changing your mindset in the way that's needed and getting to grips with the basics of money management are possible. This is not a 'get rich' scheme, but you can start to see some great results quickly if you put in the effort and take action. The first question that you need to ask yourself is: How committed are you to turning your money situation around so that you achieve financial freedom?

This book is about understanding who you are and why you are that way, so that you can break free and achieve the wealth and success that you desire. Everyone can become wealthy and happy, but only a few make the effort to turn these opportunities into reality. Reading the words on each page won't help you if you don't take action and propel yourself headfirst towards your new wealthy life.

As women, we are genetically one percent different to men, but that one percent can make a whole lot of difference if we utilise it to our advantage. At 211 degrees Fahrenheit, water is hot. At 212 degrees, it boils and generates steam. Steam can power a locomotive. One degree isn't a big measure but can be a powerful thing in the right context.

In these pages, you'll discover how to drop the excess baggage of your life. So much of how we handle our money is derived from our past, being played out time and time again. It's time to stop looking in the rear-view mirror and start looking at where you are going, so you can head in the direction of what financial success and ultimately financial freedom mean to you. Each of us has a different view of what these terms mean, and a starting point in moving forward is discovering what our definition of wealth and financial freedom looks, sounds and feels like.

It doesn't matter where you are right now with your finances — whether you're bankrupt, you're lousy with managing money or you've been unsuccessful in business. That's all in the past. Your time is now, so draw a line in the sand. Upgrading your mindset means that your past will no longer reflect how your future is going to pan out.

You'll discover that you have built up not only a glass ceiling above you but also glass walls around you, thereby confining how wealthy you allow yourself to become. Often, we think of glass ceilings as the unofficial barriers women have faced in the workplace when looking to move up the corporate ladder, but we also place these limits on ourselves. The glass walls are often put around us by people close to us and by events in our past. Your mind may have put them there for your protection. If you want to create true wealth for yourself and your family, then you need to break through these walls and move away from your current comfort zone.

Learning how to handle money gracefully and never being able to lose it once you have it are more important than having pots of money right now. Wow, that was a hard lesson for me to learn. It took several hard lessons, which became progressively more severe, and it took several years before I screamed to the Universe that enough was enough. The only advantage of being at rock bottom is that there is only one way that you can go, and that is up.

The most important lesson that I have learned is that wealth is something that happens in your heart and mind. It is how you feel. It's a relationship that needs to be nourished just like any other relationship. You can heal your relationship with money.

I'm sure that I am not alone in the desire to have the dignity of receiving enough money to be financially free. This is why I was inspired to write about the journey I've made, from being financially humiliated to being financially free, sharing how I healed my relationship with money, and the many techniques and tips I've learned along the way. I wanted to share with the world that if a girl from Yorkshire can untwist herself from a financial mess then so can anyone.

For years I've battled between the practical elements and the more spiritual elements. There are those who follow the spiritual path much better than I do, and those who follow the practical elements better than I do, but when you combine the two, the magic can really happen for even the most ordinary of folks. I use the word *ordinary* not in a negative way, but to reflect most of us. We may be unique and special but so is everyone else. Does that not make us ordinary? From here on in, ordinary should be a good and positive word without negative or boring connotations.

Ordinary women can do amazing things and achieve awesome levels of financial success.

This book is for all the women (and men) in business, who have become lost in the wilderness of money matters.

"In the long run, we shape our lives, and we shape ourselves. The process never ends until we die. And the choices we make are ultimately our own responsibility."

Eleanor Roosevelt

My Story

*I*always loved numbers, so it was no surprise that I chose to study accountancy at university. By the final year I started to struggle with anxiety, not that I knew that's what I had. It was not something that anyone talked about back then. Somehow though, I coped, and to my surprise I managed to graduate with honours and landed a job with one of the top five accountancy firms in the country.

Out of a group of 13 who started the gruelling three years of training, I was one of only four who made it to the other side and the only one who didn't have a fail on my exam scorecard. It felt like the tide had turned.

Exciting times lay ahead, or so I thought, until an illness put me off work for nearly 12 months. Returning to work was a struggle and I made it through six months before deciding I had recovered enough to look for another job. I soon landed the ideal job with a small accountancy practice, and I moved back to my hometown.

Fast forward two and a half years, and just after my twenty-ninth birthday, I was made partner. At this point, I believe I was the youngest female partner in a firm of Chartered Accountants, at a time when there weren't even many women in partnership roles.

Just before my thirtieth birthday, I left the partnership having been forced to find a way out. Luckily, we had not signed a partnership agreement at this point, as the partners couldn't agree on what to pay me if I ever took maternity leave!

Within the following year, I purchased an office building in a beautiful part of town, in addition to the acquisition of another accountancy practice. Things were going great and with the encouragement of my office co-owner, I took the professional exams to become an Independent Financial Advisor.

I was ready to explore new ideas though, so having discovered a company that coached accountancy firms I took my entire staff to their annual conference. During one session, they had a woman on stage who was talking about the fantastic things she had done to grow her practice. I declared to my team that I'd be on the stage next year. I had set my intention, and I believed it was possible.

I took every opportunity to learn and develop my practice until there I was at the next annual conference, on stage, talking. I was asked to speak at their mid-year conference as well, and the one after that. In fact, after three years of speaking at all their conferences, I did suggest that people might be fed up hearing from me!

With my growing business, I felt I needed to give something back to the community. Soon after, I saw an advert in the local newspaper – which I rarely read – asking for a volunteer to be a governor at the local college, who was preferably female and preferably had experience of finance. As the only applicant and fitting all their criteria, I was taken on.

Joining the college the same time as me was a new CEO, who announced that he wanted to expand the scope of the college and build a new campus, one which would at the time be the most money spent on an educational building. A year later and after overcoming some internal politics, I was the youngest chairperson of a UK college.

The next few years were exhausting, with relentless meetings with bank managers, funding council representatives, local officials, top civil servants from London, MPs from the surrounding boroughs and, not to mention, four different Education Ministers who each needed to be briefed on the most substantial capital build under their remit.

By this time, I was director in a company in India which was going through a buy-out; the chairperson of a board on an institution with circa £30 million in revenue, over 1,500 members of staff and undertaking a £70 million capital project; and the owner and chief executive of my accountancy practice which now had 15 team members across two offices and outsourced staff based in India. On top of all this, I somehow believed that I could take something else on.

I was offered the chance to bring an Australian/US training company over to the UK. Having already attended training sessions in the United States, I knew the concepts were the same the world over. It was an exciting time that allowed me to give presentations in places such as Sydney and Las Vegas.

I did have the common sense to hire a business coach at this stage. Hindsight screams that this should have been done years before, but better late than never as the saying goes. The coach I chose was ex-Special Forces and a recently retired Major from the British Army. As well as helping in business matters, he also got me looking at self-care and becoming physically healthy, but it was unfortunately too late and the inevitable burnout soon followed.

Over the next 18 months, the manager at my practice left and set out to destroy my business. There's a saying about a woman scorned – well, it's equally true of men. A business partner in the coaching business, which I had luckily moved into a separate entity for legal and tax reasons, also proved to be a costly mistake as he was an emotional bully who took advantage of my circumstances.

I eventually sold the accountancy practice. This was around the time of the property crash, so add into the mix my growing anxiety over money and a house I needed to vacate as I couldn't afford it any longer. I fell further into depression. I'm sure some people were saying, "How the mighty have fallen!" and it certainly was how I felt. The following couple of years were full of darkness, and I didn't pay much attention to my finances or give adequate consideration to the money that still needed to be repaid.

When the time was right to start pulling myself together, I got myself a temp job and rediscovered that I had skills. This led me to a job where I ultimately became the finance director, spending five years in this role.

For the first time I was managing money in a business that did not belong to me, and I realised that I was good at managing cash flow. It was quite a revelation, considering that my inability to manage my own cash had led to my financial nightmare. The only difference was that there was no longer any emotion involved. I had no emotional attachment to the money in the business.

It was delving into and disconnecting from the emotional side of money that helped me to turn my situation around, understand how I thought about money, and examine what beliefs I had playing in the background of my mind.

I went from having debts to having savings. It took me a few years to pay off my debts, but I did it in a methodical way without depriving myself too much. I managed to go on holiday each year, which might seem extravagant when you have debts but it's how I decided to reward myself for continually bringing the level of debt down.

After a few years, I was able to upgrade my situation, creating significant steps in my savings plan and buying a new car. I bought the new car, a BMW 1 series, for cash. It wasn't the wisest of financial decisions, but I don't list it amongst my money mistakes. It might not be the best use of such a large sum of money, but from a mindset perspective it was a huge leap forward.

Not only was I helping the business grow significantly but I was also starting to help others implement cash flow management techniques and grow their businesses and personal finances. It did feel weird, helping these people, when only a few years prior I had been in more of a financial pickle. They came to me for help regardless, knowing that not only was I adept at the technical side of money, but I had also managed to transform my own financial situation from complete chaos to clarity and calm.

Helping people create their own clarity out of chaos around money led me back to studying at the Mindset Coach Academy to become a Certified Mindset Coach.

People who knew the old me thought I was a little crazy for ditching the structure and prestige of a formal career to one where I would discuss meditations, affirmations and emotions and remove money blocks – but I always had faith. It also helped me to take the leap from my newfound security of being in employment to the thrill of being in charge again of my own destiny as a solopreneur. This time things were different. My money mindset was different and I had a solid financial foundation.

The practical side of me, born from all the training over the years, believes that you still need the practical elements to deal with money, but help from other sources is also useful. The way I thought about money and success needed to change if I was to avoid repeating the patterns of the past. The right mindset is vital.

I believe that everything happens for a reason though, and we are given specific paths and challenges to make us into the person we are today. The reason for my journey is to help you to develop a healthier relationship with money, so that you can turn your money situation around and achieve your version of financial freedom.

"When I'm tired, I rest. I say: I can't be a superwoman today."

Jada Pinkett Smith

1
Is Superwoman Wealthy?

*H*ave you ever tried to be a superwoman? Many of us are guilty of attempting to be her: working many hours at our job or in our business, going to as many networking breakfasts and lunches as possible and keeping the family home running as smoothly as it can be, while ensuring the kids get to all their activities and clubs on time.

Wow, I'm exhausted just thinking about it! It is no wonder that this fast-paced lifestyle is not sustainable in the long term. It certainly does not help you become wealthy and live an abundant life.

Even if, like me, you don't have kids, it is still a huge juggling act. When you pile on top of this already teetering heap all those activities we want to do for ourselves – see our friends, grab a coffee and take a yoga class – it should come as no surprise that burnout ensues. In fact, we often give up on the things that are for 'us'.

This pursuit of being superwoman can take you to rock bottom not only physically and emotionally but also financially, as it's all connected.

Despite being intelligent women, we still often decide that we need to be superwoman or some version of her. You've probably heard the myth that as women we can have it all; in fact, it's now expected. There is a pressure on us to constantly be more, to be better. Be more than what? Be better than whom?

Sometimes we just need to stop for a minute and think about this, rather than charging forward in pursuit of 'having it all'. Yes, work on having it all, but go about it your way, a more feminine way, a way that works for you, a way with more grace and ease and less hustle and bustle.

Is It Really A Man's World?

There is no denying it, we are different to men. We think and act differently. So why do we pursue wealth in the same way?

Perhaps it is due to the 'corporate world' where men still get paid more than women. That's the world that most of us know. We've worked in it, we know people who work in it and we see it portrayed on television and in the media.

The corporate world is set up to mirror the outside world, which is typically masculine. Certainly, for those of us in the UK, USA or Australia, we have been born into a culture that celebrates the masculine. Times are changing, but it is painfully slow progress.

The Hofstede research back in 2001 examined the masculine paradigm and looked at which countries were predominately masculine in terms of energy and which ones were predominantly feminine. They defined feminine values as those of family, well-being and collaborative working.

This research may be a few years old, but nothing appears to have changed much. Japan came out as the #1 masculine country with a rating of 95%. The UK came in at #9 with 66%, the USA #15 with 62%, closely followed by Australia at 61%. The least masculine country was Sweden at only 5%, with countries like the Netherlands and Denmark not far behind, and in stark contrast to the UK.

It's not surprising then that for those of us born into a masculine culture, Superwoman has become the archetype of our time. If you joined the world of work in the eighties or nineties, then our role models were women who were trying really hard to fit into a man's world.

In the UK, we had a female Prime Minister in the 1980s, and whether you love or hate Mrs Thatcher, she made her mark and did things her way. It was a way that was strong and focused, and certainly masculine in nature.

We also had films like *Working Girl*, which first aired in 1988. The boss character, Katherine, was a bold and self-confident woman who wielded her femininity like it was a superpower. Why not? In the film though, Katherine's character is on one hand aspirational and on the other a complete joke. No one in the film was sure what to do with a woman who was so self-assured. The same was true in real life. Even thirty years later, some people – and that includes other women – are still not sure how to handle a self-assured woman.

Back then, our role models in business were the women who embraced this feminist movement, or at least appeared to. I'm sure for some of them it was a struggle, as they were just following the crowd and trying to fit in with the men of the industry. They did all this while mostly abandoning their feminine energy. That was just how things were done at this time, as though it were the only way for women to get ahead.

When I started work after graduation, my office had one female manager, and the rumour was she was the token female in the management team. I'm not sure if this was true or not, since the same would be said even if she deserved the position on merit. Whatever the reason for her appointment, she didn't fit in at the office. She would not be out at lunch with other managers or have chats over coffee during the day. She didn't belong to the 'club' and was often kept out of the loop. I didn't want to be this woman. I wanted to be like the men, be part of the tribe.

Being like a woman was not the way ahead, even if you were a woman. It was the first real attack on the male-dominated world of business management, and it's what these women needed to do and become in order to make the way for future generations of women in power and wealth.

These women needed to make a bold statement so that they could get noticed. The problem was they started to believe that in order to succeed in business or to climb the corporate ladder, they needed to conform to the more masculine version of themselves. I was that woman, following those I saw as being successful. What I didn't realise at the time was that I was giving up my power as a woman, and that this power is one that has actual substance and shouldn't be discarded but yielded for the good it can do.

Many women around my age are taking back this power that they had previously given up or lost along the way. It most definitely is a superpower, and one that should not be discarded like trash.

We can be equal to men, but we don't need to be masculine to do it. Our difference is a strength which we can utilise for our advantage. We need to embrace this difference and find a new kind of power to be the woman that the world needs. Working with these differences, rather than discarding them or fighting against them, allows us to be in flow with our purpose.

Finding Our Superheroes

If you want to become wealthy with grace and ease, you need to embrace your feminine values while still operating in a world that has different values. The new generation of female entrepreneurs are grasping this concept, but those of us who are a little older still find ourselves stuck in the masculine world that we grew up in.

The traits often associated with the feminine energy are things like connection, empathy and nurturing. These traits are associated with just 'being' while the masculine energy traits are associated with 'doing'.

Each of us, however, has access to both energies. We need to find a balance between these energies, and we cannot be balanced when we choose to ignore our feminine energy. Not being balanced means you aren't you, not the 'real' you anyway. We are designed to need that balance in order to feel whole.

I love the book written my Mary Portas, *Work like a Woman: Manifesto for Change*. Mary played the corporate game for years at a very senior level, abiding by the rules set by the men. She became tough, competitive and aggressive, which are all pre-requisites to compete with men at their own game.

Like many women who adopt these qualities and allow them to take over, her innate feminine qualities of natural energy, instinct and sensitivity were hindered. She suppressed the superpowers of being a woman, and like many of us she did this until she was absolutely unable to do it anymore.

What does all this mean? When we give up some of our feminine energy in order to succeed, we lose some of our innate power. We forget how to be a woman, and that saddens me. I'm sad for myself, that I lost my way and ignored this energy for so long, because how we act at work inevitably overflows into our personal lives. It's not something we can switch off when we leave the office. We then start to feel unbalanced, become stressed and stay stuck in a job or business that doesn't feel right to us.

Some women have successfully embraced this way of working. They are the next generation of female leaders, in senior positions in multi-national organisations, creating their own global businesses or even leading countries. They are successful because they have stepped into their feminine ways.

Even if, like me, you have worked the 'masculine' way for a long time, you can change. It is safe to change. There are others who have set the pace for us to follow. You just need to believe in your power as a woman.

Those who break records and achieve what seems impossible never cease believing in themselves, even when everyone else thinks that what they want to achieve is impossible. Roger Bannister was an athlete at the time when everyone believed that it was not humanly possible to run a mile in under four minutes. Roger ran in the 1952 Olympics, and although he broke the British record for the 1,500 metres, he finished fourth. Yet, he still believed he could break the four-minute mile, and in 1954 he ran the mile in 3 minutes and 59.4 seconds. His record only lasted 46 days, because now everyone knew that the mile could be run in under four minutes. In fact, in the coming year, the record was broken several times.

To become a new upgraded version of superwoman, you don't need the kind of belief that Roger Bannister had, as you won't be the first with your background and skills to become wealthy. Instead, be like the others that broke the record in the year after Roger, believe it is possible by knowing someone else has achieved what you desire. You can now locate people who can become your Roger Bannister and allow them to show you the way forward by following them on social media platforms, reading their blogs and their books and maybe, if appropriate, taking their online courses or workshops.

Emulating role models is a must for self-improvement. We have a need to thrive for a standard set by others or have a benchmark to compare ourselves to.

One of the most profound turning points in my personal development and my career path was embracing and exploring being a woman in business, in my own unique way. It was the belief that women can succeed in business without sacrificing their inherent female qualities, and looking up to the new generation of female entrepreneurs who were shining the light on how to do this.

Mapping Out Boundaries

It's a tough job to create this necessary balancing act in order to be able to forge ahead with making money, whether in a job or on our own, and at the same time maintaining the 'home' life we also crave. Even if you don't want to follow the social norm of a partner and kids, it's still a juggling act.

I am talking about that seemingly elusive thing, commonly referred to as the work-life balance. It is a fabulous concept that has become associated with the superwoman persona. In my humble opinion however, it is a phrase that needs striking out from modern vocabulary.

The phrase itself conjures up several negatives for many women. Women who strive for success are often reminded of the price of working. Society reminds us, but we also constantly remind ourselves.

As a concept of balance, it is something worth pursuing. If we are creating a new way of working for women, then surely it will allow us to have some form of balance, right?

We need to stop judging ourselves by society's standards and create our own. Define the boundaries that work for you and stick to them. Otherwise, it will be like creating a budget for allocating your funds each month, then buying what you want when you want. Spend more than you earn and, guess what, you'll soon burn out financially. Eventually, any line of credit that has allowed you to continue with this folly will cease to exist.

One of the major keys to success, whether financial or any other kind, is knowing your limits. If you keep pushing yourself, being the first one in the office and the last one to leave, raising a family and looking after a home, following the mantra of work hard and play harder, it won't be long before burnout hits. And when it hits, it can really punch hard.

We can avert burnout by setting ourselves a few boundaries. Even if you haven't decided on what your wealthy future will look like, and we'll be exploring that later, there are some boundaries that you can implement immediately.

Protecting Your Work Time: No matter how many or few hours in the day you can work while still juggling all your other responsibilities for the home and family, you need to get strict about sticking to those hours. It doesn't matter if it is two hours every other day or four-hour days, those hours need to count. Every minute needs to count.

Don't get sucked into social media or do the washing during work time or agree to meet a friend for coffee and cake. These are just distractions. Friends won't appreciate the fact that you have working hours you need to stick to if you don't tell them. They may not understand if they aren't a business owner, and that's fine, they don't have to, although most friends will get it when you explain it to them. "Sorry, I'm at work then," is enough of an explanation. Let's face it, that's probably all you would need to say if you worked for someone else.

Friends and clients who are mums can only work on creating their wealth between the hours of 9:30 a.m. and 2:30 p.m., the end of one school run and the beginning of the next. There are many women who do this successfully. They often can't work any more hours, unless they plan to work after the kids go to bed or in between the cleaning, washing and ironing. What these women do is know their boundaries, then find ways to do what needs to be done without compromising their physical and emotional health.

Slice Up Your Time: Be crystal clear on what you're going to do and when. Carve up your time into meaningful slices and allocate your work activities accordingly.

I find working in 90-minute cycles suits me well, with half-hour breaks in between, but you can carve up slices of any duration that works for you – 20 minutes, half an hour or an hour – it's your time, so you should slice it as you like. Choose a period, then divide and assign your daily tasks, client appointments, etc., to these time slots.

Important Tip: Remember to create a time slot to deal with your finances regularly. You need to monitor how you are doing financially and make changes to any products or services that are performing well (you want to put effort into selling more as well as ditching those that aren't profitable).

Also, allocate some time in your diary for YOU. A burnt-out woman is never going to make any money!

With your newfound boundaries, you can start to mould yourself into your own version of superwoman and work on creating that elusive balance.

Embrace It, Release It, Increase It

"Whatever women do, they must do twice as well as men to be thought of half as good. Luckily, this is not difficult."

Charlotte Whitton, Author

It took many years after my financial crash to realise that this feeling of unbalance between my feminine and masculine energies had contributed significantly to how I was feeling at the time, which had resulted in the poor decisions that I constantly made about money and my business. I had all the practical skills where money was concerned, but the 'unbalance' was significant enough that I ignored a lot of things which should have, all things being equal, been routine in nature.

One way this unbalance shows up is when we see other women as threats. I wasn't the only one feeling and acting this way. I've seen many of my female friends who climbed the corporate ladder struggling to deal with those women who were higher up, or indeed, the strong independent women in their own team.

Being in a position where you find it hard to connect to others, because you don't know who you are, is a sad place to find yourself in. You believe you are the only one.

When we are mostly using our masculine energy, we can easily burn out. In fact, women have a higher burnout rate than men. This is because we act like men and push hard like they do, despite being women. It comes down to biology. Men have reserves of testosterone that they can use to help them push through and work harder, whereas women don't have these stores to fall back on, so we use adrenaline and cortisol to help us. When our body keeps using these stores and depletes all reserves, burnout is the next port of call. In fact, it's the only place left for us to go.

It is not our fault, we were just built this way. Irrespective of whether you are in business, are a stay-at-home mum or have a job but no kids, we can all risk getting into a state of burnout if we run around doing a hundred and one things. We need to stop. Overscheduling our time does not necessarily lead to a wealthy lifestyle.

A key skill to master, and it's a tough one, is to slow down. In case you need it repeated:

s l o w d o w n

One of my clients, Catherine, was well on her way to burnout. She ran two businesses and had a child in nursery school along with a stepdaughter to care for every other weekend. Her husband worked away during the week. Although between them they brought home six-figure incomes, she didn't feel wealthy and her lifestyle didn't feel abundant in any way.

"You've got to be kidding!" Catherine declared when I suggested she explore slowing down. "I need to be earning more money, not less!" All this stems from the belief that we need to work hard to be wealthy, a belief that many of us pick up when we are kids.

Were you ever told that you needed to work hard at school if you wanted to get a good job? Or perhaps that Dad is working late because we need the extra money to get luxuries such as going on holiday? All seemingly innocent things that were told to us as kids can come back later in life to haunt us. Do you say similar things to your children?

For Catherine slowing down became a priority, mainly because her best friend had just hit the burnout zone and she could see the same worrisome signs in herself. She figured that earning a lower income by working less was better than having her earning capacity be reduced to zero. The family could not thrive on just one salary.

This is not one of those sugar-coated stories. I won't tell you it was easy because it wasn't, but over a period of six months, Catherine reassessed every aspect of her life and business, got her finances in order, budgeted wisely and became smart about how she spent her money and how she organised her business. At the end of six months, she was working only two-thirds of the earlier number of hours but for the same amount of money. A year later and she's working the same number of hours, but it's not as stressful, and she's earning nearly twice as much money.

Catherine is not any different to you, so if she can do it then so can you.

Research by McKinsey & Company, called *Centred Leadership: How Talented Women Thrive*, says: "It's about having a well of physical, intellectual, emotional, and spiritual strength that drives personal achievement and inspires others to follow." In other words, as women we need to embrace our feminine energy and use it to our advantage.

Mrs Doubtfire – Fiction Or Real Life?

Asking for help can be a challenge for those who view themselves as smart and capable. We don't want to be considered weak, when really the only person thinking that is ourselves.

When you are constantly hitting a wall and feeling tired and frustrated that you aren't progressing, you need to take some time to analyse how you got into this position. Be completely honest with yourself. When you do this, you'll find your limit in this area. Don't keep banging your head against a brick wall, instead choose to learn where the wall is and find ways to avoid it.

Not all of this help will be free, depending on the type of help you're asking for. It's wise to outsource tasks that free your time to earn more money. Sometimes, you have to take that leap of faith and pay for the help before you see the return on investment.

Hiring a cleaner for a couple of hours a week could free up valuable time. You can then use this time to fit in more client work or maybe to develop a side hustle that will help you earn more money and eventually leave your stressful job.

If you're in business, then the list of tasks to be outsourced is endless, and you should pay special attention to areas you currently procrastinate over or don't have the skills to do the work effectively. Marketing and accounting are prime examples, so are the plethora of admin tasks that small business owners need to undertake. Start making your list today.

Whether you are employed or self-employed, there are bound to be areas where you can get help for a reasonable fee. So, as you work on yourself and prepare your mind for your new wealthy life, take some time to discover what help you will need along the way. It will get you to your destination quicker and less frazzled.

We have been led to believe that working harder equals more money, which in turn equals more happiness. This is a lie. A big fat lie! In fact, this is one of the most common limiting beliefs among women who unconsciously allow this belief to hold them back somehow. It's a no-win situation. You want it all, you 'need' to have it all, so your unconscious mind gets you working hard, too hard. Then you are exhausted, you don't get the results, so you work harder and do more, as you want more. It's a vicious cycle that's often hard to break.

It's not about working harder. It's about working hard and being smarter. More money doesn't automatically equal more happiness. In fact, for many women, having more money often equals more stress – stress in dealing with the money and keeping up with the new standard you've set for yourself.

The good news is that you don't need to be superwoman to be wealthy. You do, however, need to work hard as well as work smart to become wealthy, but that doesn't involve pushing yourself to the brink of destruction.

Become Your Own Super-Hero Character

"Think like a queen, a queen is not afraid to fail. Failure is a stepping stone to greatness."

Oprah Winfrey

You can gift yourself some abundant superpowers to help you along the way and make life a little easier.

Superpower one: Becoming comfortable around your numbers and understanding how these numbers are aligned to your goals is a superpower, and it's one that's fairly easy to master. You don't need to become a financial whizz-kid, you just need to grasp the basics and create a plan for your money by knowing where you are now (i.e., your net worth, the sources of your income and where you spend your money), where you are heading in terms of savings, and what your future income will look like, then creating a budget and having a plan for eliminating any unhelpful debt.

Okay, I know that all this must sound scary to some women, but this is stuff you can learn how to do in a day, and then with a little practice it will become second nature. That's when it becomes your superpower.

Superpower two: You may have heard about the Law of Attraction and that it is possible to manifest whatever you want. You truly can – I do, my friends do, my clients do. I've seen other people do it too. But we didn't manifest stuff by sitting on our bum all day sending out orders to the Universe and expecting the rewards to be delivered directly to our door. We worked at it, we put in effort. The key is to work smarter and work with the Universe, but you do need to work and sometimes it will be hard.

It's utterly crazy, but people are generally more willing to delve into how they can get the law of attraction to work for them than they are about getting to understand what their numbers are telling them. Both these ideas are important if you want to create a wealthy lifestyle. The first superpower gives you the confidence that you can handle being wealthy, and the other provides magic-like assistance in giving you what you desire.

You probably have other superpowers you can tap into, that are not related to money but will help you build the wealthy lifestyle you desire. As you read this book and uncover those powers, make a note of them. That is the beauty of your mind – you can recreate yourself.

All of us have superpowers that give us the ability to be financially independent and create our own version of financial freedom. Relying on someone else, including your partner, is gambling with your future. Being out of balance is not a sustainable strategy for long-term financial stability. The only truly viable financial strategy is for you to take control of your own financial destiny.

Reflections:

- ➤ How do you see yourself?
- ➤ Do you see yourself struggling to be superwoman, trying to keep up with this mythical persona?
- ➤ Do you feel like you are wandering through life, trying your best, but with no real purpose or financial strategy?
- ➤ Are you embracing your natural energies?
- ➤ Have you embraced the superpowers that are in your armoury? Do you know what they are?

Affirmations:

- ➤ It is safe for me to create money boundaries.
- ➤ It is safe for me to use money to create an easy life.
- ➤ I am enough.
- ➤ I am worthy of having the life of my dreams.

"Your vision will become clear only when you can look into your own heart. Who looks outside, dreams; who looks inside, awakes."

CARL JUNG

2
It Starts With YOU

Successful people are just ordinary folk who know their strengths, weaknesses and beliefs along with their purpose and what motivates them. They have clarity in all these areas, and they know how to tap into them and use them to their advantage.

It's the same when creating wealth. Those who are successful tap into their strengths and weaknesses when deciding how to handle money and how to create wealth and link their money-making activities to their purpose.

Unfortunately, many people choose to blame the money and not themselves for their lack of financial success. Money is just the tool; it doesn't have a mind of its own and has no opinion on whether it thinks you are worthy of accumulating money. It's a fact: Your current financial position is down to you and so is your wealthy future.

It is also critical to become aware of your *Core beliefs and values*. This self-knowledge can help to steer you through the twists and turns and odd detours you will no doubt encounter along the way to wealth and prosperity.

For many of you, this will be a deep dive into uncovering what really makes you tick. Profound shifts occur, which can be scary, but as you become clearer in your vision you give birth to your greater self.

The Big Question

It takes some time to get clear on who you are and how you think about money. It took me a few years, and even now I'm in a state of continuously revising and updating my thoughts as I smash through each new glass ceiling. Sometimes new glass ceilings appear rapidly, in a relentless stream of obstacles. When you are on an upward trajectory, then this is only to be expected.

There is no get-rich-quick scheme or a click of ruby slippers to get you to your destination, but don't let this put you off. You will be working at your job or in your business in any case, so why not spend some of that energy on understanding yourself?

The headliner question you should be asking yourself is: "Why is money important to me?" It is the very first question that I ask when helping anyone start their financial empowerment journey. It does not matter whether you are working on the more practical side of money or purely looking at the mindset work, you should always start here.

As a money coach, it's my all-time favourite question as it gives me an instant understanding of how tuned in someone is to their purpose and aspirations for the future. It's the start of a deep dive into discovering what my clients really want from life.

Unfortunately, most initial responses to this question are generally vague, with the top choice being financial freedom. That is why people want money. Of course, each of us has a unique definition of what financial freedom means.

What does financial freedom mean to you? Have you ever stopped to think about this and spent time journaling your answers? You've got to keep asking yourself "Why do I want this?" and "What does this look like? Smell like? Feel like?" so you can start to really drill down to what financial freedom means to you.

We get more out of life when we know our purpose and live in accordance with fulfilling this purpose. For some, this purpose is evident from an early age. A friend at school knew he was going to be a pilot from a young age, and he joined the Royal Air Force on leaving the education system, became a pilot and is now flying for a large airline company. None of us had any doubt that this was going to be the role he embraced as a career.

I, on the other hand, fell into my first profession as an accountant. Banking was my original choice, aged ten. I liked numbers and maths, and a family friend worked for a bank, so it seemed an obvious choice. And let's face it, most kids don't know what an accountant is. Pursuing my studies at college, I then fell into accountancy, deciding to study the topic at degree level. I liked it well enough, but it wasn't my purpose in life. I stayed in the profession because I was reasonably good at it.

Like many women, it was only once I reached forty that I started on my journey to a new career. It wasn't a complete switch, as I loved money and numbers. The transformation from accountant to wealth mindset coach took nearly ten years. It takes a lot of deep digging to find out what your purpose is in life, and for some, this goes beyond merely finding the vocation that will fulfil us.

Have you ever heard the saying "do what you love, and you'll never work a day in your life"? It's not just a saying that looks good on a social media meme, there's truth in it too. When you become aligned to your purpose, what you do each day to generate more income no longer feels like work. The journey to get there is a long haul, but you learn so much on the way about yourself as well as life itself.

You don't need to have this conversation with anyone else. To begin with, it can be between just you and your journal. The prompt you start with is "Why is money important to me?" Continue journaling until you have a detailed description that you can make happen in reality in order to live your ideal life.

Finding YOU

"Observing yourself is the necessary starting point for any real change."

Chalmers Brothers

Many of us do not really know ourselves very well, despite inhabiting this mind and body for the last however many years. Most of our thoughts and habits are dictated by our unconscious mind, so we are not aware that they are playing on repeat in our mind, continually directing us. This came as an enormous shock to me, when I first started to delve into sorting out my money issues.

Who we are, how we think and how we perceive what is happening to us and around us creates the foundation for building a wealthy mindset.

Can you answer these questions?

- Who am I?

- What do I believe in?

- What is my purpose?

- What fills me with joy?

Seemingly innocent questions when you first read them, but when you give yourself the time you deserve to answer them you discover how deep and meaningful the answers become. Only recently have I begun to fully understand my answers, after half a century on this planet, and I must admit that getting here has been extremely difficult. So no matter what age you are right now, it's an opportune time to start exploring your responses.

Whether you choose to just read the questions, have a go at answering them, or really introspect on your answers over the coming months is up to you. I'll just ask you this: "How badly do you want to become wealthy?"

The work involved in self-reflection is not easy to undertake for many people. I used to see many blank faces when I asked my clients. Hopefully, that is not you, but just in case it is, here are four questions that will serve as a launch pad to begin your journey of self-discovery.

Start with these even if you have done loads of self-reflection work before. I always find them useful journal prompts when I'm ready to look deeper before going to the next wealth level.

What is your sixty-second personal elevator speech? If you're in business and go to networking events, then you will have no doubt spent some time working on this for your business, but have you ever worked on this in relation to your personal life?

If you are the owner of a micro or small business, then you are probably thinking that your business is your personal life, but that is not the case. You need to acknowledge that your business is just a tool to allow you to follow your purpose and to allow money to flow to you. It's a tool, just like money.

Friends in recruitment tell me that this is probably the most important yet poorly answered question in job interviews. Oh boy, I've heard some real rubbish in my time as an employer, and all that it ever told me was that the potential employee was either just feeding me words that they thought I wanted to hear, or that they had no real clue.

Please don't dismiss the importance of this question. It's not about creating a statement but being able to know precisely what your life is about and where you are heading.

What are you passionate about? Following a passion of any kind is a good thing, and you need to pay attention when it appears because it indicates an area of life that you need to devote more attention to and do more of. Passion can be related to areas in your work or more generally tied to pursuits in life.

What or who would you be if you knew you couldn't fail? Seems like a standard question that's asked by many business coaches and one that you may well have previously considered. It was one I originally shied away from, but there's a reason why so many coaches ask it.

The risk of failure terrifies most people. It paralyses us into taking no action and convinces us that staying put is the best way forward. Burying your head in the sand where your money is concerned certainly isn't a sound financial plan, yet it's one that many women and men are quite happy to adopt. Think about it. No risk of failure. How liberating would this be? If you were 100 percent certain that you could be or do anything you wanted and not fail, what would be your answer?

If money were no object, how would you live your life differently? Many people equate happiness and success to the amount of money they have. How many times have you heard someone say, "If I won the lottery, I'd.........."

Remember, this question isn't really about money at all. It's more about thinking outside the limits we tend to put on our aspirations and actions because things seem out of our reach financially.

You may not be able to do those exact things, but once you know what your true desires are, you can expand your thinking and begin to develop a plan to work towards goals you may never have imagined possible. How cool is that?

All four questions are tough, and the answers may not come easily or quickly. I'm re-evaluating mine on a regular basis. This work is hard but necessary in order to really understand yourself on a deeper level. Whenever I take the time to work on this area, I achieve further breakthroughs and get deep insights.

Getting to Know YOU

"The only way to do great work is to love what you do. If you haven't found it yet, keep looking. Don't settle. As with all matters of the heart, you'll know when you find it."

Steve Jobs

Although you do need to get to grips with some financial basics, the real key to creating the wealth you desire lies in changing how you feel about money, wealth and success. How can you change your feelings when you don't know who you are?

You can take better care of yourself financially than anyone else can. Don't be fooled into buying into the notion that others can do it for you and make you rich. I learned this the hard way, and oh boy, the price tag was way too high. As the American financial expert Suze Orman says "You can't fix a financial problem with money, you can only fix a financial problem by fixing yourself."

Do you really understand who you are, despite having 'known' yourself all your life? Do you know what excites you, what you stand for, what your passion is in life and in business? We often think we know, but do we really? Getting to know yourself means taking time for self-reflection and staying committed.

Digging deep into what makes you tick is damn scary. It takes courage to break through the fear of what we'll uncover. Often our biggest fear is whether we will actually like ourselves when all the truths are laid out in front of us, when we have nowhere to hide. We may be pretty and nice on the outside, but rotten at the core. Highly unlikely, but then that's what fear is, it's irrational. If it's not the fear that's holding you back, then it's the lack of willingness or motivation to dig deep.

Why would you want to? Well, if you want to live at ease and create the wealth that you desire, then you need to understand where you are coming from and what is important to you. There are circumstances when educated guesswork is enough, but this isn't one of those times. This is the time for becoming as clear as you can possibly be.

You may well be thinking, hang on a minute, I picked up this book because I want help with creating a wealthy and abundant life for me and my family, but this doesn't sound like it's about money. Well, if you want money for the sake of wanting money, then you did indeed pick up the wrong book.

But if you want to create a life that fills you with joy, where you're able to create all the money you need to sustain the lifestyle that allows you to live with passion and purpose, then you did pick up the right book, and you need to start working on yourself no matter how uncomfortable that makes you feel. While a wealth mindset isn't enough in itself to create wealth, it does make the process easier.

If you discover and embrace your true passion in life, you'll never have to struggle for money. Find the 'love' in your life and have the courage to go after it. When you know what your true purpose is in life, you won't see money as something that can purchase happiness. You'll start to see money as just the tool that gets you there.

My financial quest wasn't a journey I expected to go on. It has felt like a quest at times, perhaps not to the intensity of Frodo Baggins's – there have been no mystical creatures or exploding volcanoes – but it has been a voyage of discovery, slow and deliberate, certainly nothing like jumping on a motorway and travelling from point A to point B as quickly as possible. It's a country road where there are weaves and turns, sharp bends, some U-turns, followed by some stretches of road where you can put your foot down.

The good news is that at times you can find it an interesting journey if you are willing to relax and enjoy it. You may become so enchanted with the fabulous scenery that you may feel compelled to make frequent stops to immerse yourself in the splendour.

If your goal is to achieve financial success sooner rather than later, then the key is to keep moving forward, making as few stops as possible. It's okay to slow down sometimes so you don't miss out. Your version of financial freedom is the place you want to be at, so no matter how comfortable and enchanting the scenery looks along the way, always keep your destination in mind.

There is no point starting the journey if you don't know where you'd like to end up. Yes, you might get there, it is possible, but you need to face the fact that the odds aren't great. I don't know about you, but I like to increase my chances of success wherever possible. You want the odds stacked in your favour.

It was for this reason that I embarked on my journey of self-discovery. It has taken a while, and I'm still working on the finer points, but I've found that the more I understand myself and what I really want out of life, the easier it becomes to attract the wealth I need to get there.

Starting a Financial Pilgrimage

If you are ready to go on your financial pilgrimage, to set out on the quest to reach the wealth and financial freedom that you desire, then start by discovering your core values and beliefs, becoming aware of your strengths and weaknesses and uncovering what really motivates you.

Core beliefs and values play a huge role in how we navigate our lives, irrespective of whether we realise they are playing a part in the navigation or not. Often we don't, as they operate in the background of our unconscious mind. This process is often started through journaling. I was never keen on this notion of journaling and resisted the need to journal for the first few years of sorting out my wealth mindset.

I was eighteen when I first tried to write down my thoughts and beliefs, but soon after that my mum discovered and read my diary. Following this incident, keeping a diary of any kind lost all appeal. It's a shame, as I now look back on life and wish I had been able to journal, in order to get my thoughts straight and avoid taking some disastrous detours. Not that it is my mum's fault. Most definitely not. It was my responsibility, and mine alone, when I decided not to put thoughts to paper.

So if you have any preconceived ideas about journaling, I urge you to get over them as quickly as possible. While working on your mindset around money and wealth is more important than writing in a journal and saying positive affirmations, these are great activities to start out with and cost very little, unless you are a stationery addict!

When you start to journal, discuss with yourself the highs and lows of your past, particularly in relation to money.

These high and low periods is where you will see the core beliefs and values that steer you. They lead you to your highs and take you away from the lows. It's when situations trigger emotions that our values show up.

You need to understand your *strengths (i.e., skills and capabilities)*. Most of us, and I certainly include myself here, find that producing a list of weaknesses is an absolute breeze but putting together an equally impressive list of strengths is a formidable task. A great way to get to understand your strengths is to ask people who know you. Not too long ago I was sitting in a business retreat and we were undertaking this exercise, personally and in relation to our businesses. I was quick to admit that my list of strengths had only a couple of things on it. I was certain I had more than two strengths and it was frustrating not to be able to articulate them.

This is why it's good to continually surround yourself with other women (and men too) who can raise you up and have no reservations in telling you how marvellous you are, because I was bombarded with a whole string of strengths from everyone in the room. Others tend to see our strengths far more easily than we do in ourselves.

You can of course ask anyone – your best friends, parents, siblings, spouse or children. Take a little of that courage that you have within you and just ask them. Remember that your biggest critic and the person who is the meanest and cruellest to you is you yourself. Don't dismiss what they say, and make sure that you take notes. Take plenty of notes.

What *motivates* you? Why do you get out of bed in the mornings when you don't need to go to work or feed the kids? It's a sad fact but we often get out of bed on autopilot, because there is so much stuff that we need to do. We need to take care of those around us who need a helping hand and we need to earn enough money to pay for our basic requirements such as food and shelter. If there was no one depending on you for their needs and you had all the money you could ever want already earned in the bank, what would get you out of bed then?

From a journaling perspective, this is about mapping out an ideal day in your ideal life. Visualisation might be more your thing, and you can with a little practice create a movie in your mind of your ideal day. A movie that's in technicolour, with surround sound, which feels like an exciting place to be. Play this movie to yourself again and again, whenever you have time during the day, as the last thing at night and as part of your morning routine.

For each 'showing' of your movie, make sure that you ramp up the volume, turn up the colour and ensure the movie is right there in front of you, like you're your own personal cinema, and that you're seated in the front row or even actually feature in the movie.

As you work on improving yourself and becoming clear on where you are heading, money will become more than something you need. It will become a bridge leading towards your true purpose in life.

You need this self-knowledge to navigate the twists and detours you'll no doubt encounter. It really makes me sad that so many people live their lives in automatic mode. Remember, you were put on this earth to live your life with passion, to find and fulfil your true purpose.

Without a true understanding of ourselves, we tend to look to the past rather than to our aspirations to guide our lives.

Living By Your Own Values

You cannot and will not be able to know yourself until you take the time to be still. Many people don't know themselves because any sort of silence scares them. You'll know you are one of those people, if you never want to be alone or don't feel comfortable when you are alone. You might not want to admit that the reason it's so uncomfortable to be alone is because you have every flaw staring back at you.

It isn't until you get alone, evaluate yourself and are completely truthful with yourself that you're able to see every facet of your life—the good, the bad and the ugly. Be courageous, stop and be quiet, spend some time on your own and discover your true self. Realize who you truly are, not who you want to be or, worse still, who you think others want you to be.

You may already have a set idea of who you desperately want to be, but it might not be who you were designed to be. This is why knowing who you really are is so important.

When you know who you are, you will finally see where you and your specific gifts fit into the bigger picture.

And although there are many points along your journey to help you discover yourself, the best way to begin is to take a personality test. These self-evaluations aren't perfect, but they do pinpoint your top areas of strengths, so you can focus on the change you were meant to bring into the world. There are many such tests out there.

I use the Sacred Money Archetypes® quiz with my clients and while it is specifically designed to gauge how your personality deals with money, it's also useful when applied to the rest of your life, because how you deal with money is how you deal with life. You will find a link to this quiz in the resources section at the back of the book. Taking the values test by the DeMartini Institute is an insightful experience too. The questions really make you evaluate yourself even if you have already spent some time doing this work.

Find what you are good at and, just as important, what you are not good at. Another potentially difficult step in the process of finding who you are, but it's a necessary one. Sure, it takes trial and error to find what you're good at, and no, I don't want you to give up before you've had more than enough attempts, but knowing when to quit is a gift that everyone needs to learn. There is definitely a fine line.

Quit when you've put in ample time and your efforts aren't giving you any returns. I certainly wouldn't have gotten into a financial pickle, or at least nowhere as deep in the mud, if I had left my business before it deteriorated completely. The danger signs are usually there, waving a huge red flag in front of your face. But you don't see these flags, like I didn't, when you are going through life on autopilot.

The next question is "What is ample time?" Only you can decide that. Every situation and every person is different. But when you quit correctly, it isn't giving up, it's making room for something better. Of course, if I hadn't gotten into such a financial mess and then dragged myself out of it, then I wouldn't be living my purpose now and helping my coaching clients to heal their relationship with money.

I wish I could say that discovering this purpose was instant, but it took me time to realise this. Generally speaking, when your actions do nothing but drain you, rather than produce more passion and increase your drive to do more, that's a good sign it is time to turn your focus somewhere else. Your strengths will show you who you are.

Ask for feedback. If you don't know yourself, hearing what others have to say about you is a helpful practice. Ask them two simple questions: "What strengths do you think I need to develop further?" and "What weaknesses do you think I need to work on?" Of course, their opinion isn't going to be perfect, but their feedback will probably indicate a few areas you should at least take a second look at. This step is especially important for those who are struggling to find themselves. Sometimes those closest to us can see things we might not be able to see in ourselves. Make sure that you ask more than one person. Everyone sees the world and the people in it in different ways. Obtaining just one person's viewpoint will give you distorted feedback.

A large chunk of knowing yourself can be uncovered in your relationships. Realising that you'll never truly know anyone else until you discover yourself can reinforce the importance of knowing yourself. This rule also applies to any relationship in your life, including the relationship you have with your money. Almost as much as you need to know yourself, other people also need to know who you are. People need to know the real, authentic version of you.

Ready to Make The Big Changes?

Those who are able to make the biggest changes when it comes to creating wealth do so by understanding the mechanics of money as well as how they think about it. They also understand themselves and are in the process of creating a life where they live in alignment with who they truly are.

An amazing transformational journey kicks off when you start to uncover who you really are, where you want to go, and by what means you plan to get there.

Reflections:

- ➤ Why is money important to me?
- ➤ Who am I and what do I believe in?
- ➤ If money were no object, what areas of my life would I change?
- ➤ What does financial freedom look like for me?
- ➤ What is the purpose of my life?

Affirmations:

- ➤ I accept myself unconditionally.
- ➤ I have the power to change my world.
- ➤ I am in alignment with my soul's purpose.
- ➤ The better I know myself, the clearer my purpose becomes.

*"If we did all the things
we are capable of doing,
we would literally astound
ourselves!"*

Thomas Edison

3
Go Big, Go Bold

Where are you headed? It's a question most folks don't know how to answer or are unprepared to dream big enough to answer, yet everything is possible. I'm not talking about the general destination of financial freedom, but the exact coordinates.

As the saying goes: "The future belongs to those who are willing to believe in the beauty of their dreams." So, believe in your dreams! Your unconscious mind is powerful, and it can make your dreams come true. You just need to give it some direction.

This is where your belief system is likely to kick in. You could be thinking, "Fabulous, I'm ready to go, but where do I start?" which is fantastic. Or, you could be thinking something like, "Yep, my unconscious mind is not that powerful," or "I'm sure this can happen for others, but not for me." Park all the negativity right here. Also park any other negative thoughts such as "I am not good enough" or "I am not worthy" as we'll be discussing how you can start to remove these thoughts later in the book.

You may be a wonderful and unique woman, but what makes you think that you are so special that your unconscious mind will work in a different way to everyone else's?

Now is your time. Time to go big! Feel the wind in your hair and the freedom of the open road as you take control and ramp up the speed.

What A Girl Wants

An empowered woman not only knows what she wants from life, but also has the courage to ask for it. She knows where she will live, whom she will spend her time with, what they'll do for work and leisure activities, and where she will travel. She knows this in such precise detail that if she described her destination to you, you would be able to imagine it as if you were seeing it on a big movie screen in technicolour, with the surround sound cranked up to maximum.

Her dreams are big and bold, so much so that they fill her with excitement for what the future holds, helping her to stay positive as she navigates the typical twists and turns of raising a family and running her business. These dreams aren't there to allow her to walk around with her head in the clouds; they are there as a reminder of her destination, so that every decision she makes pulls her towards her dream life.

When negative thoughts creep in – and let's face it, you cannot be 100 percent positive all the time so they will creep in – she can use the big dreams she has been nurturing to help her explore and overcome these doubts. When you don't know where you are heading and are just going through the motions on autopilot, you are not aware of limiting beliefs, so they keep you small and confined inside your comfort zone.

One of my favourite quotes, which is attributed to Confucius, is, "If you shoot for the stars and hit the moon, it's okay. But you've got to shoot for something." Personally, I dream of becoming a *New York Times* best-selling author, which would allow me to spread my message to thousands of women around the world, empowering them to take charge of their businesses and money so they can attract the abundance they desire. Having this dream led me to write my first book, then another, and now I have this book. Even if this book were only to sell 500 copies, that would mean I achieved more than if I hadn't ever followed my dream.

Empowered women don't just wake up one day and know everything they want in immense detail. I'm sure some people can sit and meditate and then, hey presto, they can journal their way to figuring out their purpose and ultimate dream life in forty-eight hours. They're probably those lucky few or those 'gurus' who are selling their coaching services on social media.

Of course, it would be nice if we could all find out our purpose quickly, so we could get on with pursuing the dream. But like with many other things in life, getting there takes time. You need to have a little faith, let go and trust the process. When I began this process, I was at a complete loss as to what I wanted from life. This state of mind was likely the reason I was in a mess, financially and mentally.

You need to start dreaming with what seems plausible for you. Don't worry about making grand plans – they will come later if they are, of course, what you desire.

As you take each step and get closer to what it is you ultimately want, remember to keep your mind open to new possibilities. You might be thinking, "Yep, I understand that, but it is easier said than done!" I know I struggled with finding my dream, my purpose in life. For this Yorkshire lass and many 'normal' folks, it's a little bit more complicated than it is for 'gurus'. It took ages before I was in a position where I was ready to put the plan together. When you're ready, you will take the steps that I mention in this book, and if you're not ready yet, well, you'll know what to do when you are ready.

For now, be open to the fact that you can dream big. Go ahead and give yourself permission to do so right now. What do you have to lose? Once you have cultivated the mindset of being ready to dream big, you can take the next steps, one at a time.

Next Steps

You might be living your life without fulfilment or a deep satisfaction in the things you do and the things you have. If this is you, then you are not alone. There are also those of us who are somewhere between being unfulfilled in the present and being certain of our dream for the future. While both scenarios are common, we should not let life continue to be this way.

Settling for the status quo won't get us what we want, so why not go in search of your purpose in life? At some point you have to take control of your life and find that one thing, whatever it may be, that brings you satisfaction. You need to find your purpose in life for this to happen.

Having a purpose is what keeps you going and pushes you to want more for yourself. I was forty-six when I arrived at this stage, and I have taken my time working on this purpose. My coaching clients are typically in their forties or fifties. If you are younger but already seeking your path, then you are ahead of the game.

What do you do when you are not at that point in your life? One thing is for sure: don't worry or stress about it. That never helps, just like waddling in a pool of misery does not help. Not having worked it out yet is an okay position to be in. Don't let anyone convince you otherwise. Life is a journey, whether you have the map or not. Having the map allows you to get to your ideal destination, that's all. So, what can you do if you are at the point of not knowing what your purpose looks like?

Cut the self-sabotage: Being mean to yourself doesn't serve any positive purpose, nor does it help you figure out your purpose any quicker. All it does is hold you back. Try reframing your self-sabotaging thoughts and behaviours to help you become more relaxed about your current situation.

You start this process by literally asking yourself questions to get a better understanding of how you are self-sabotaging.

"How?" and "Why?" are good questions, and while the questions are short your answers will be more in-depth. You should do this questioning in your journal and not in your head. Conversations in your head, when it comes to sorting through emotions and beliefs, won't be robust enough to get to the bottom of what is going on.

When you have some thoughts on paper, look for evidence of how these beliefs are true, as well as evidence of how they are not true. Make sure that you carry out a thorough analysis of how your thoughts are not true – such signs will be out there, although they may not be obvious at first.

Now reframe your thoughts to something that is more realistic, and then practise replacing your negative self-talk with this more realistic reframed version.

Accept that you don't have it figured out: It's okay to not have your life's purpose figured out at this moment in time. No one is born knowing exactly what they are here for or how they are meant to be living their life. Some of us take years to get to a position where we can figure it out, because we need to go on a journey to gain the necessary experience and knowledge we require. Don't worry about everyone else. Some people may seem like they have everything figured out – but they may or may not in reality. Our perceptions of others can be misleading or completely false. Not that it matters, because you just need to be concerned with yourself. Accepting where you are at will help you move on with more ease, which will help you figure out your purpose sooner rather than later.

Know that things will change: You may not be where you want to be just yet, or you may not know where that ideal destination is for now. That's okay, but it's worth reminding yourself that it won't always be this way. The key is to start working on your purpose today. If you do that, then you will set the tone for the future. Focus on the fact that you can influence your future, and the further you go down the path of self-discovery and make small changes, the further you will be able to travel. Ask yourself this: Would you rather take a long time reaching your ideal location (even when you don't yet know what it looks like), or not make any effort in finding your ideal location and risk never being able to get there?

Financial Goals

Whenever I mention the term 'financial goals', people's eyes glaze over. They know what goals are and often set some, even though the approach may be less than effective, but with the word 'financial' thrown in front as a prefix, people often react like I'm speaking in a foreign language.

Here's the translation: Financial goals, sometimes referred to as financial targets, are just goals that are expressed in monetary terms. For example, to reduce credit card debt by £10,000 in the next twelve months; to save £50,000 into a tax-efficient retirement fund in the next 36 months; or to create a fund of £6,000 to support you in six months' time when you switch from employment to self-employment.

Some of these financial goals will be based on your stepping stones, but others will represent your ultimate idea of financial freedom. By setting financial goals, you are quantifying your ambitions.

Financial goals let you know where you are going by determining, in money terms, how much you need to save. They help you work out strategies for getting to your version of financial freedom. As with all goals, setting them is the first step to achieving them! This is the first hurdle, so do everything you can to get past any resistance to setting goals. After all, you don't win the race by missing the first hurdle. Start to quantify your lifestyle choices, houses, cars, etc., into your financial goals.

Do you already have a vision board? Many people do. Is it up to date? Is it online or on paper? It needs to be one of these options and not just inside your head.

If you don't have one, there are vision board workshops out there to help you. Not all workshops are created equal, but you'll still have a fantastic time putting your vision board together. You can either start with your vision board and turn it into financial goals, or you can think about your goals and then interpret them into a vision board. It really doesn't matter which way you go about this, so long as at the end of the day you have a set of financial goals that, when you achieve them, will give you the life you desire. Financial goals are just goals that have a monetary value attached to them – that's the money you need to transform your dreams into reality. It's easier to generate income when you know what you want the money for, not in a desperate way, but when you know how you will use the money in your new wealthy life.

Many people are going through life believing that they cannot afford their ideal lifestyle, yet they have no idea how much that sum would actually be. Perhaps it won't cost as much as they expect!

Knowing the cost of something doesn't make it expensive or out of your reach; instead, it allows you to make plans and set goals to ensure you are able to start living this life at some time in the future.

So how do you cost your ideal life? How do you calculate the monetary amount needed to be earned each month to support this lifestyle?

The first step is to create a list or use your vision board to record the key components of what you'd like in your ideal life.

What type of house would you be living in? Is it the one you're living in now? Would you be downsizing? Would you want a bigger house or the same kind of house in a different location? Become specific about what kind of house you see yourself living in.

Think about how many holidays you would take each year and the type of destinations that you would go to. Perhaps you want to go skiing once a year, plus some winter sun in the Bahamas and a cruise around the Mediterranean.

What kind of hobbies would you pursue? What kind of activities would you participate in?

Would you be working full-year or part-year? Or would you just spread your work out around your holidays?

What kind of car would you be driving? Would you have two cars for the household? Or would you prefer to take a taxi everywhere? Would you have a chauffeur?

Think about how often you'd be eating out and the kind of places that you would be going to, perhaps for the weekend, plus the spa day with your girlfriends!

You will no doubt want to reserve some of your time for activities such as spending time with your family, which will not cost you any money but just require the freedom to be able to take time out. You can have that as part of your vision for your ideal life, but when it comes to financial goals you only need to be concerned about the things that will have direct money values.

Ideal Life Valuation

So many people are chasing the notion of a six-figure business or a £10k-per-month business, but these are arbitrary amounts that mean nothing to your unconscious mind. One of the most misquoted money-related sayings is that "money is the root of all evil" when, in fact, it is the love of money that is the root of all evil. I doubt if it's the root of *all* evil, but there is some truth in the saying. Your unconscious mind and the Universe will not direct you towards opportunities to bring in money just for the sake of it. Wealth is so much more. It's about having the money to support a lifestyle that allows you to do the things you want to and have the freedom and choices you desire. Of course, if funding your ideal life takes £10k a month, then go ahead and use this as a financial goal.

When you have your list, the complete list, not the version that you think is achievable and not extravagant, the list with all the things that you truly want, then you can start to put a cost to the items. You need to know the annual cost, so for example, if you are planning on going on one cruise every two years, then you need to know the price of that cruise, split the cost in two so you can begin to save in year one. The internet is your friend here. You can get the price of just about anything from information available on the web.

When looking at the price of houses, work out the mortgage cost each year, or perhaps the rental value of the type of property you want, as this will give you a cost per month. When you know what the monthly cost is, you can work out the annual cost just by multiplying it by twelve.

When you have the total of all the annual costs, you can add in your normal expenses from your budget or by reviewing how you currently spend your money. It will of course need adjusting slightly for your new circumstances, as a larger house will cost more to heat and your clothes allowance may need to increase in line with your new travel plans. Be as realistic as you can, even when working with your best guessed estimates.

Then there is just one more annual figure to include and that is for your long-term saving. You still need to make plans at this stage for your retirement.

Add all the three annual amounts together, and that's going to tell you how much you actually need to earn per year to pay for your ideal lifestyle.

This amount that you need to live on is not the amount you actually need to earn in your business or from other sources, because the taxman would want his share before the money comes to you. So the amount you've calculated is the amount you need to earn after tax. And that's the amount that comes into your personal bank account and into your pocket.

We need to adjust that up to the amount you actually need to earn before you pay the taxman, because that's how much money you need to generate in your business or from other sources of income. So how do you do that? Well, there is a little bit of maths involved. Take the amount that you need in physical cash each year to pay for the things that you want, and divide it by hundred percent minus the percentage of tax.

It's going to be best if I explain this by putting some figures in, so let's say £180,000 per annum is the cash coming in to your personal account that you can actually spend. You are going to give the taxman 50%.

Doing that calculation, you work out that you need to be generating profit in your business or from other sources in total of £360,000 per annum. So you can pay the taxman his 50% in the various guises they want that money, through tax and National Insurance. That would then leave you with £180,000 to spend. I know that seeing these kind of figures can be scary for a lot of people, the realization of just how much you need to pay the taxman.

But, you know, paying tax is a fact of life. You can of course legitimately reduce the amount of tax you pay, and I would suggest hiring an accountant to help you with this. Quite simply, if you generate a good income, you are going to have to pay the taxman.

Now work out what this equates to per month. What are you aiming for? In the example, this equates to £30,000 per month that you need to be generating. When you work out this figure, it's so much more meaningful to you than, say, plucking out the arbitrary £10,000 a month, £25,000 a month, or £50,000 a month, whatever it is. This number actually means something, the figure that you're then working to is actually going to give you the life that you want.

Stepping Stones

Now, you may be thinking, "Well, this is my ideal life, it's going to cost me £30,000. The way my business is now, no way could I ever scale up to that!" But you have got two choices here. You can just work and use some of the tools that I'm going to be discussing throughout this book to bring that money to you. Or you can expand your business to a level where it accumulates that amount of money, because it is possible. It is entirely possible to use both options together too. Whatever it is that you want in life, you can get it when you put your mind to it and start using these universal laws.

But it also might be that you're thinking that's too far into the future, and that you'd like to cast a mini version of your ideal life like a stepping stone. Maybe you're in a two-bed house and your ideal house is a four-bed one with a swimming pool. Maybe you can see an in-between level, you know, a three-bed house that's detached in a nice area, or even a four-bed house on a housing estate. It is not quite where you want to be, but it's like a stepping stone. If that is what you need to do to create something that feels more realistic for you, then go ahead and do that. Knowing your initial point and the cost of your ideal life lets you determine what the stepping points are in your income goals.

Don't be afraid to get specific. The more specific you can be about your goal, the easier you will find to put a cost to it. Reach for the moon and miss, and you land amongst the stars. You've probably heard this before, but it's true. I know landing amongst the stars would be my preference to not having tried at all or only having tried half-heartedly.

So that house you've always wanted, do you know where it is located? How much will it cost you to purchase it? How much will it cost to fit it out in your chosen style? Get to know your numbers. Price up the life you want. You don't want to be telling yourself that you can't afford that. It is easier to believe a goal is attainable when you know the amount of money associated with it, even if you are not yet able to spend that amount of money. Knowing the amount actually helps to take away some of the fear.

Even if your dream house seems unrealistic, there is nothing wrong with having it on your vision board. How do you know what will be unrealistic in your future? You can, of course, aim for a stepping stone, a more realistic house that is somewhere between where you are living now and where you ultimately want to end up. It can be quite difficult, even for those with great imagination, to believe we can live in that big house by the sea with a private pool area when we are living in a rundown area in a two up, two down terrace. Anything is possible, but sometimes we may want a little help. Perhaps it is more believable for you to envisage living in a nice four-bedroom property in a nice area of town. Just don't dismiss the ultimate goal. Even if you end up spending your days living in the lovely four-bedroom house in the nice part of town, it will still be a whole lot preferable to continuing to live in the bad part of town.

Upgrade one level at a time, so long as you don't just aim for the next level up. If you're used to travelling in the economy seats on the plane, it can seem unrealistic to think that you can just jump to purchasing first class tickets. It's quite a hike in price; an economy return ticket with British Airways in 2019 from London to Sydney cost £840, yet a first-class ticket cost £5,502. If you aren't ready to upgrade just yet or can't see that you will ever be able to reach first-class travel, then your stepping stones would be to first upgrade to premium economy at £1,500, and then to business class at £4,402. You can do this with all areas of your life, not just travel. You might even be surprised to find that you already have the first-class versions in some areas of your life.

The practical side of my brain constantly tells me to reign in a little from my wildest fantasies, but that's okay, because I know that with some good planning and a dose of success, anything is possible if I don't take my eyes off the final big goal.

It's important to have a vision so you can continually take small mindful steps towards that vision. If something knocks you down then you might be out of the game temporarily, but when you are ready to join again you know exactly where you are and where you are heading. You don't go back to square one.

Your vision acts just like a magnet. The clearer the vision, the more you draw the right people and opportunities to you to ensure that the vision pans out. This is essentially how the Law of Attraction works, it helps you see more clearly. It is pointless if you're unable to see the right people and opportunities just because you don't know they are right for you.

Inspired Action

To be wealthy, you must get your priorities straight. You do this by setting goals. I like the Pablo Picasso quote "Only put off until tomorrow what you are willing to die having left undone" because it gets right to the point.

Life is shorter than we expect. I still can't believe I'm fifty; that time went pretty quickly. Time goes by fast whether you are living on autopilot or actively working out what is and isn't important to you. Taking action, starting with figuring out where you want to go, gives you a better chance of getting there.

I have never failed because of a lack of opportunity or from having inadequate abilities. You, no doubt, will be the same. We fail because we are not sure of our real goals. We make half-hearted attempts to achieve goals we don't really want, and then beat ourselves up when we fail or barely get by.

Taking inspired action is not about creating a plan of action, although you will need one of those as well. It's a phrase used with the Law of Attraction. It is saying that you need to chase your dreams because sitting on your bum doesn't bring results. Create the team, create the vision, work on your skills, set your goals and GO!

Reflections:

> What would your ideal life look like if money were not an obstacle?
> How are you self-sabotaging your efforts to achieve what you desire?
> What are your top three to five financial goals?
> How much will your ideal life cost you?
> Can you put any stepping stones in place, to help you on the way to your ideal life?
> What three actions will you set for yourself to help you reach your ultimate goal or next stepping stone location?

Affirmations:

> I am driven to achieve my goals.
> I am focused and determined to achieve my goals.
> Everything I want is within my reach.
> I always have more than enough money to meet my needs.

"What you think, you become. What you feel, you attract. What you imagine, you create."

Buddha

4

Think Yourself Wealthy

*E*ach of us has a unique view of the world, including how we view and define wealth. The 'programming' that we receive in our early years helps to form the perceptions that we have about money, wealth and the people who have or don't have money. Having these perceptions is like having a pair of prescription glasses for our mind, which allows us to see, or not see, certain events and opportunities.

Here's the good news: You can change your prescription. You don't need a lot of money to develop or maintain a healthy attitude towards it. Review any recession that's hit the modern world and you'll find that those who were not wealthy but living within their means, with a good attitude towards money, were able to survive even when times were tough. Then there are those people who live beyond their means and despite earning good money (over £100,000 per year) can suffer financial ruin when recessions hit. It happens, I was one of those people, and believe me, it was real and extremely painful.

In order to create the right foundation for a wealthy and stable future, you will need to retrain your brain to adopt new habits and skills regarding money management and wealth. You need to change your glasses, if you want to see the world with clarity. As an adult, that is possible if we choose it to be. If you are willing to put in the work and use the techniques available, you can start to think yourself wealthy.

Sometimes, we don't just want to throw a pebble into the pond and make a small ripple, we want to be able to jump in and create waves. This is possible if you are prepared to do the work and change the way you think.

Reboot Your Mindset

It's not known how much of our mind's power we use, but experts in neuroscience are certain that we can reprogram our thoughts. When it comes to money, this is fabulous news.

Have you ever been working away on your computer when it starts to do weird stuff or completely freezes? What do you do? Well, unless you are a tech wizard, you're likely to hit the reboot button and once the machine is running again, you'll delete any offending files or programs. Sounds familiar? I think even tech wizards adopt this approach!

You can do this with your mind. The more you tell your mind to do something, the more likely it becomes that you will be able to do this activity as a matter of habit. I remember when I was learning to drive a car, I would sit there wondering how the hell I would ever be able to remember everything and drive with confidence. We do learn, though, through repetition, the same way that we learn things when we are studying.

Research into how the brain works has shown that our minds cannot distinguish between memory and fiction. This is why visualisation techniques are powerful tools. If we fill our brain with images of the life we desire – succeeding in our business, climbing the corporate ladder, accumulating wealth itself – then our mind can't distinguish between whether this is a memory or fiction.

Simply put, if your mind believes that you are already successful, your thought processes will shift to creating more positive and productive beliefs and habits.

If you are already a dreamer, a visualiser, then you're well on your way to putting this powerful tool into action. You can learn to be a dreamer, one who dreams with purpose. Of course, visualisation is more than mere dreaming; I like to think of it as the more advanced version of dreaming. You are more than just the viewer and the lead actor, you are also the director of your dreams, giving them purpose.

Our thoughts are the stuff of dreams and nightmares. They are the raw materials we use to create everything in our lives. Unfortunately, our minds have been programmed over the years, as a self-protection mechanism, to be pessimistic. This is why we have limiting beliefs. But where did we get them from? Who gave them to us? Do they have a logical basis?

Positive or negative changes in the way we think can cause a ripple effect, which can have a profound impact over time. If you want to start giving up limiting excuses, it is important to acknowledge that every single passing second of every day gives you the power to do something different.

Learning how can be fun. It can also be a challenge. We are never too old to learn. I never thought I was too old at fifty to become a Certified Mindset Coach, but I did have the belief that it was going to be hard to study to such a high level at this age. Once I cleared the belief, the whole process of learning the new skills and techniques became so much simpler. This does not mean that the techniques are simple, just that they were no longer out of reach and became a joy to learn. My mind suddenly started to absorb the information more readily and the whole process of learning became more enjoyable.

The first belief that you will probably need to adopt is that you are capable of being wealthy. Once you know as a fact that it is possible, your mind starts to work in weird and wonderful ways to make it happen. You stop being a victim and start entering a phase of empowerment, which is where you'll develop all the right beliefs to enable you to become wealthy.

Perception Is Key

How we interpret situations and make assumptions about life underlies our actions and steers our life. Our perception is based on our own values, beliefs and life experiences. We interpret what we see and give it meaning and then call it reality. This is basically why we all think differently.

At the time of writing, here in the UK, we have just concluded the final elements of the Brexit debate in parliament. There have been so many different views, and many heated debates on social media and among family and friends. Everyone thinks they are right. They are right, of course, in their view of the world. Others with the same qualifications and understanding of economics and politics have completely different and opposing views. They are right too, in their view of the world. Our beliefs create a filter through which we see the world, which is unique to us.

It's not just in politics that we need to constantly try to decipher and make sense of what is going on. Police officers know this all too well. They can have several witnesses to an accident, and each one will describe what happened in a subtly different way. This is why the police like to collect as many statements as possible, so that they can piece together all the different views and decide what was likely to have occurred to result in the accident.

We can become aware of how our own belief system affects us and therefore consider how others might see the same situation quite differently. Take a piece of chocolate cake. My nephew will immediately think it looks delicious, my cousin who is a cookery teacher will consider the quality of the ingredients to form her opinion, and my sister-in-law who is a diabetic will see the cake as a potential problem. All different views but just one piece of cake! Even those reading this book will see the same words, but what they each perceive the words are saying will be somewhat different.

This is also true when it comes to our money. Your point of view or perception of money and wealth can differ substantially to that of your siblings, even though you were brought up in the same house. Each of you will have had different influences outside the home and overheard the same conversations but at different ages. My brother is four years younger than me, yet if you didn't know that we were brother and sister and just looked at our financial paths, you might be forgiven for not realising that we are related. I have taken risks (not always well advised), made loads of money, lost loads of money, spent beyond my means, and been consumed with accumulating material things, so much so that my financial relationship has in the past been very rocky, nearly ending in divorce at one point. My brother, on the other hand, has had a steady rise in income, invested wisely in his business, never got into debt that he couldn't manage, and has been able to spend without jeopardising his financial future. Why? Different perceptions on how we interpreted what we saw and learned about money in our younger years.

Ask yourself: "What is my perception of money, and people who have money?" Be truthful, this is just between you and your journal.

Go to your inner circle, your nearest and dearest, and ask them to complete the sentence: "Money is ...." You'll get a variety of responses.

What You Think Is What You Become

Our internal dialogue, that ongoing conversation we all have in our heads, is the driving force behind every success story and behind every failure. Our thoughts are the stuff that make our dreams as well as our nightmares. We need to choose wisely so that we end up with the dreams. The difference between who you are and who you want to be stems from your thoughts. Once you start to change your thoughts, you will immediately start to change your behaviour.

Financially successful people ask the right questions of themselves. Instead of asking "Why is this happening to me?", they will ask "What can I change in order to get what I want?" It's a subtle difference but one that has a huge impact.

Developing a wealthy mindset is not just how you think about money. It's so much more than being about money in its basic form. It's how you trust yourself to handle your finances, how you manage your money goals, how patient you are, whether you have the courage to hit the pedal and move forward, how willing you are to learn new techniques and skills, and how well you maintain your focus and stay positive.

Choosing to be positive and having a good attitude will determine a lot about your life. If you set your mind to positivity, it can go a long way. Instead of giving yourself reasons for why you can't or shouldn't, give yourself reasons for why you can and should go for it. Write in your journal all the reasons you can be wealthy and then give yourself permission to pursue them. If you ever become stuck with what to write about in your journal, you have your answer here.

There is a part of your brain, the hippocampus, that forms your short-term memories, and if it deems these memories to be valuable to you, it will transform them into long-term memories. With regard to money and wealth, this can work against you as your negative memories, such as a business venture that went sour or a business that collapsed or investments that crashed, can be formed into long-term memories. This will stop you from obtaining success in the future, unless you can give this part of your brain some positive memories of financial decisions that have paid off. Take time to work out what you have done well with your finances, such as creating a business that was in profit, climbing to the top of the corporate ladder, making shrewd purchases or snapping up genuine bargains. Whenever you remember a good financial decision, make a note of it in your journal, and then remind yourself of all these good decisions on a regular basis.

Also add in a good dollop of logic to counteract the emotional punch in the face associated with the negative financial experiences. For example, "My business didn't fail because I was bad with money, my business failed because I didn't exercise enough control over my staff and ensure that robust systems were put in place and followed." It doesn't have the same negative impact on future business endeavours as believing that you are no good at running a business.

A woman who's living her true purpose and creating a wealthy lifestyle knows the importance of her mindset. Possibly more than any other single factor, your mindset determines your success in life, and that includes dealing with money and how much financial success you create. Wealthy people do things differently, they think differently, they perceive circumstances differently, and they certainly act in a different manner. Most importantly, they have learned that financial success starts in the mind. They know that they need a healthy 'wealth mindset'.

Ninja Mindset

A winning money mindset involves getting to the truth of what makes you tick where money and wealth are concerned, and learning to see your financial problems as challenges.

It involves digging deep, facing the truth about how you think and feel about money, warts and all, and accept that you are responsible for these thoughts. Creating the right mindset will allow you to explore the opportunities that come your way, which will help you build a successful career or business and start the journey towards the abundant life that you desire.

When it comes to your current financial position, you are the perpetrator and not the victim. This is a hard pill for some to swallow, but it's a fact that you need to accept. My financial downturn was brought to the level it reached by a property market crash, an unscrupulous business partner, etc., but if I had control of my finances and was working to a plan, then these external influences would not have had the same impact. This makes me the perpetrator, not the victim. Analyse your current financial position and take responsibility for it. As soon as you start accepting how your actions have led to your current circumstances, you can start taking full responsibility for your future potential for success.

I first learned about developing the right mindset years ago from a coach who was helping me cope with an expanding business. Dave was ex-Special Forces. These guys know a thing or two about mindset; it's what they use to survive the many battles and dodge the many potential deaths that come their way. Over the next few chapters, I'm going to take you through some of the things that I learned from Dave and how I adapted them to rise up from financial disaster to financial fitness.

No matter what situation you get yourself into, it's your mindset that plays a huge role in helping you climb out of those darkest moments. I was lucky in a way when I started my financial fitness quest as I had the money management side of things sorted, so I only needed to apply the techniques and knowledge! The new lesson was in creating a ninja mindset that was going to deliver the results I wanted. When you change your mindset, you change the world around you.

You get yourself into a financial pickle when you are spiralling with negativity. If you think negatively, then that is what's going to happen – something negative. There is no real satisfaction here in knowing that you were right.

Doing anything great requires courage, in order to push through the fear that always has a way of showing up when we are ploughing forward or changing any part of how we operate. Courage does not mean being unafraid; having courage and showing courage means facing your fears and saying, "I may be scared but I am moving forward anyway."

Courage is like a muscle that you can strengthen with use. Becoming wealthy requires courage. Unless you were brought up in a wealthy lifestyle, creating a wealthy life will be new to you, or perhaps you have had it before and lost it, so there is the fear that you may lose it again. You may well need to leave behind friends and loved ones who are happy being an automatic pilot. You can't expect them to want to change the way they think and act, just because you have taken the decision to do so.

To do anything great, you also have to be able to trust yourself and believe in your capabilities. A wealthy life is not something that just happens by itself, it's something you create. You must have the confidence to banish any negative voices in your head that are saying things like "People like us don't get ahead" or "Money doesn't grow on trees" or "Wealthy people aren't nice and aren't liked." Don't give up on the things you believe in, on the life you have decided to create for yourself and your family, and most importantly, don't give up on yourself.

Of course, knowing what you want and being willing to do whatever you need to do in order to attain it are two extremely different things. Knowing your goals keeps you motivated. Remember, if it doesn't challenge you, it won't change you. Set high goals and don't stop until you reach them. Climbing a mountain isn't easy, even for experienced mountaineers. Ascend one milestone at a time, ensuring you are heading in the right direction and taking the shortest route possible.

Just because you are struggling doesn't mean you're not learning. Every failure has something to teach you, and everything you learn helps you grow. If you are unwilling to learn, no one can help you; if you are determined to learn, no one can stop you.

Every great success requires some kind of struggle, and good things really do come to those who work hard and struggle to pursue the goals and dreams they believe in. To radically change your life, you have to change yourself. Start building your new mindset today – think the thoughts that will help you move towards your goals right now.

There's a fine line between knowing when to move forward and knowing when to stand still. The most successful people do all they can to move forward, but they also have the patience to wait and watch. Those who are impatient tend to lose out on great opportunities. Sometimes you must wait for the right thing.

One of the worst setbacks that can happen is losing focus and allowing procrastination to step in. Important as it is, it's also difficult to stay focused and disciplined. The best way to maintain your focus is by staying in the here and now and concentrating on everything going on in this particular moment. Distraction wastes time, and procrastination keeps you from moving forward. Discipline is the bridge between goals and accomplishment, and a mindset of focus builds that bridge.

Scarcity or Abundance?

I first learned about the concept of a scarcity mindset from Stephen Covey's book, *The 7 Habits of Highly Effective People*, where he says: "Most people are deeply scripted in what I call Scarcity Mentality. They see life as having only so much, as though there were only one pie out there. And if anyone were to get a big piece of the pie it would mean less for everybody else."

Many of us, unfortunately, exist in scarcity mode where money is concerned, maybe not 100 percent of the time, but as a general modus operandi.

This scarcity mindset revolves around the idea that there simply isn't enough money to go around. When it comes to dealing with their finances, someone with a scarcity mindset will focus on the short-term implications of every decision that they make. I see this particularly with how people spend their money, as they are not thinking about the future. They are usually the kind of people who are living pay check to pay check, whether they are employed or self-employed. They also tend to be quite jealous of people who have money and feel very negative and sad when things don't come to them. They perceive their money woes and lack of wealth as somebody else's fault. Remember what I discussed earlier about taking responsibility and not being a victim? You will probably be able to think of some people you know that live out their entire lives stuck in this mindset. You might even be one of them! If you are, all is not lost as you can switch your thinking, which you will need to do if you intend to create and keep any significant amount of wealth.

The opposite of a scarcity mindset is an abundance mindset. Covey says: "The Abundance Mentality, on the other hand, flows out of a deep inner sense of personal worth and security. It is the paradigm that there is plenty out there and enough to spare for everybody. It results in sharing and it opens up possibilities, opportunities and creativity."

Typically, the abundance mindset focuses on the longer term and is accompanied by the deep understanding that just because you don't have something in your life right now, it doesn't mean that you can't get it at some point in the future.

From a money point of view, it is much easier to deal with your finances when you have an abundance mindset, because you don't feel the need to spend money as soon as you get it and you're able to plan for a wealthier future.

The key is switching from a scarcity mindset to an abundance mindset, and then cultivating that mindset. It's not something that happens overnight, but it is something that can be done.

Let's explore further some of the main differences between those with a scarcity mindset versus those with an abundance mindset. Those with an abundance mindset are known for thinking big and not putting limitations on their mind, which helps them set high goals to be able to achieve their dreams.

Those with a scarcity mindset believe that there are limited opportunities out there and only so much wealth. You will find them saying things like, "I can't afford that" and when you say things like this every day, it reinforces the belief and forms that exact situation in your life, stopping you from living abundantly.

Someone with an abundance mindset is much more likely to be optimistic and is generally happy for those around them who are achieving success. If you can, you should spend more time with these successful people, because after all, as the saying goes, "You are the sum of the five people you spend most of your time with."

A person with an abundance mindset understands that change is an integral part of life, and that when it comes to finances they may need to change the way they talk about money and wealth with others. A person with an abundance mindset will embrace and accept this change, whereas somebody with a scarcity mindset will be plagued with fear. Fear, as we saw in the last chapter, is commonplace, but we can choose whether we are startled like a rabbit in the headlights with this fear or whether we embrace it and move on.

Someone with a scarcity mindset is always going to choose negative thoughts and adopt a victim mentality, which creates stress and anxiety, as well as more fear, worry and resentment. Their daily focus will be on what's not working rather than what is working.

There are some subtle changes that you can make very easily to switch from being in scarcity mindset mode to abundance mindset mode. As you go along with your abundance mindset, then over time you will accumulate more of the positivity around having such a mindset and it will become easier for you.

The choice is yours to make, and it's a simple one – scarcity or abundance?

Make Your Choice

Abundance! I am sure that is your choice. Deciding that you would like to have abundance rather than scarcity is an easy and quick choice to make. The key though is changing how you think so that it supports the choice.

This is work that does not get done in a flash. With professional assistance, you can change your mindset from where you are now to one of abundance thinking in as little as 28 days, but that takes commitment as well as an investment of time and money. Or you can do this work on your own. This takes time though, so be prepared for that. It has taken me years of working on my own.

Everything you desire is possible, no matter where you are starting from financially or what kind of family you were brought up in or what level of education you have.

Reflections:

➢ Will you do the work necessary to change the way you think about money?

➢ Are you ready to give up all the excuses, blaming and complaining?

➢ Will you take full responsibility for your future, giving up all the victim stories you have been using as a crutch for most of your adult life?

➢ What is your perception of money? Is this perception going to help you achieve your ideal life?

➢ In what areas of your life do you already feel wealthy?

Affirmations:

➢ I love my luxurious, wealthy life.

➢ I am living a life of abundance.

➢ I deserve to be financially free.

➢ I am comfortable changing my money mindset.

"You can use a challenge to awaken you, or you can allow it to pull you into even deeper sleep."

ECKHART TOLLE

5
Leap Over The Hurdles

*U*nless you've lived in a vacuum all your life, you will have made mistakes that haunt your decision-making abilities and beliefs, which limit or block you completely from moving forward and ultimately achieving the financial success you desire. Don't let your past mistakes be an excuse for not realizing your goals and aspirations for the life you want.

You have a choice: learn to leap over these hurdles or stay where you are. The great thing about life is that there's always a choice you can make, if you want to.

As women, we have more than our fair share of money issues and worries. It's not that men don't worry about money, they do, but it's usually in a totally different way. Most of these worries have deep-seated roots in our past, and stem from a part of our past that we need to release even if we cannot forget it. To do this, we need to take some time to examine our past relationship with money so that we can re-frame it to our advantage.

There's an Arab proverb that states that you should write the bad things that happen to you in the sand and then they can be quickly erased from your memory. It is a nice idea, but most of us prefer to have the terrible things that have happened to us engraved in marble, especially us women; therefore, our painful memories remain immortalised in our minds. This is true of all the bad stuff that has happened to us, but it seems to be particularly true in relation to our money decisions.

The great news is that you don't have to walk around with your financial failures and mistakes shackled around your ankles weighing you down. You've probably heard the saying "don't dwell on your past." Dwelling on the past does you no good, but that doesn't mean you shouldn't look back in order to examine why you did what you did and understand how it is affecting you in the present day. You can then release the past, stand firmly in the present, and prepare to step confidently into the future.

Habits of Destruction

How do we get into such a pickle with our lives and end up in the position of being our own worst enemy? It's not just one situation or a set of circumstances that takes us to this position. We pick up all sorts of beliefs that we don't realise we are collecting, which ultimately build up a huge defensive glass wall that holds us trapped in our current situation.

We don't pick up these limiting beliefs overnight. They start to become implanted in our unconscious when we are a child and then get re-affirmed time and time again throughout our adult life.

Sometimes these beliefs work against us. For example, when trying to create a successful business, our belief that having money (the very thing that the successful business will give us) might make us unpopular among our current friends and family will keep us from becoming successful. Our conscious mind and unconscious mind are working against each other. It's like having one foot on the accelerator and the other on the brake. Even if we become successful, it is likely that we either keep running into obstacles or keep spending or losing our newfound wealth.

Self-help for some is enough, and is should certainly be a starting point. By becoming aware of your limiting beliefs and talking them through, you can make sense of it all, and once this happens everything becomes more manageable.

Journaling is also a useful tool. Most people have tried journaling several times, and I'm certainly included in this cohort. It is a worthwhile exercise to persevere with, as it helps with your ability to identify and manage your emotions around money, whether that's having loads of it or dealing with the consequences of not having enough. I made such huge leaps forward when I swapped my morning routine of checking social media and emails with writing in my journal instead. Sometimes I write whatever comes to mind, rather than on a certain topic, and when I look back, it's very random and quite weird stuff, but that's okay.

Even though you've been asleep for eight hours, your unconscious mind has still been whirling away in the background, coming up with solutions to your problems and identifying the activities that will take you closer to the opportunities and people that will lead you down the next steps on the road to building your wealth.

If you're in doubt about what to write, then journal about what your ideal life will look like in as much detail as possible. Describe what your ideal day consists of, from where you spend the day to who you spend it with; how you feel about money; or what your early money memories are.

When you work out what beliefs are holding you back, you can stop them being the driving force for what is happening in your life. For each limiting belief that you uncover, consider exploring your answers to these questions in your journaling practice:

> ➢ Where did I learn this?
> ➢ How do I live by it now?
> ➢ Is it helpful or limiting?

One of the key beliefs that my client, Karen, had was that she was just no good when it came to numbers. She learned this from failing at maths in school. No matter how hard she tried, Karen always seemed to have to work harder than her friends just to get a pass.

This belief repeatedly showed up in her life as she mismanaged her money. There is often a strong perceived link between being good with numbers and being good with money matters. She had also tried to constantly collect academic achievements since leaving school, to try and prove everyone wrong, but she never quite got there, never completing any studies, and thus creating a self-fulfilling prophecy that she was no good at academic matters and no good with numbers and money.

Is such a belief helpful? It pushed her to achieve, work hard in all areas, but also left her continually struggling to feel good enough. It stopped her from being her true self. It exhausted her.

By reframing how we think, we can turn these beliefs into an asset for ourselves. Our beliefs can be reframed into something that's genuinely more productive and resourceful.

Common Limiting Beliefs Affecting The Money Mindset

I'm not good enough (or I'm not worthy). Often this results from a situation where you were made to feel inferior as a child or were told you were not good enough or weren't as good as XYZ. It can also be a culmination of a whole host of small seemingly insignificant situations where you somehow made the massive leap to concluding that you are not good enough.

I love what I do, but it's not about the money! This will keep you average rather than being successful in your business, and not as wealthy as your ideal lifestyle requires you to be.

> **If I want to make more, I'll have to work harder.** By allowing this belief to have hold over you, you use it as an excuse for not achieving what you want.
>
> **No one likes me!** Everyone has flaws and sometimes people tend to point these flaws out at the worst possible times. The problem with this limiting belief is that it becomes a self-fulfilling prophecy, because as you believe that you don't deserve friends or relationships, you don't make the effort to find them or work at them, and so those friendships or relationships don't get off the ground.

Just Proof You've Been Trying

Money mistakes are pretty common. A low-key but common money mistake is 'buyer's remorse'. Most women have suffered from this at some point in their lives.

Some mistakes are not as obvious. For me, getting into debt was clearly a mistake, but it's the little errors in judgement along the way that need to be examined.

The mistakes you've made are often an act of misguided judgement or simply something that you have done incorrectly. If the mistake arose from an error, then consider if the error was due to incorrect information or not paying attention at the time of your decision making. There is usually more to the story than just having made a mistake.

The key to dealing with mistakes is to not beat yourself up about having made them. There should be a statute of limitations on regret, but instead the guilt around the mistake tends to linger. You make a mistake and ouch, it hurts emotionally as well as in the pocket. Then you feel horrible, and its double ouch.

Forgive yourself. What happened was just one piece of your life. Making mistakes is just part of the process of living. A child stumbles, falls over, cries for all of sixty seconds and then is back on their feet ready to surge forward and doesn't think about the fall again. This is one lesson from our childhood that we need to take notice of and incorporate into our adult life.

Find the silver lining. You can do this by asking yourself the questions:

➢ What did I learn?

➢ What new actions can I take to stop making the same mistakes again?

Focus on your abundant future where money will flow freely to you and you'll be able to keep hold of the money and control how it is used. Then take yourself through the pain and examine your money mistakes.

Remember, when it comes to making money mistakes you are not alone. There are some of us who have made spectacular mistakes. Have you ever bought a house you have never seen, in an area of a city that you've never travelled to, only to sell it one year later for a slight loss without ever having stepped a foot inside?

No? Just me then! Yes, this is a true story, you cannot make this stuff up. My property developer friends were restructuring, and all the finance work had been done on the house by the same bank that I was using at the time. It took just a ten-minute phone call to the bank to get all the paperwork swapped over to my name, and another similar call with the solicitors, and a couple of weeks later I had acquired a property. In fact, I acquired two, but at least I visited the other one before selling it later.

This was a mistake, not because I lost money, but because it was irresponsible of me to buy two properties that I didn't have time to develop, to buy them without seeing them and without ensuring that the investment fitted in with my plans.

Hopefully, this story has made you feel better about any possible money-related mistakes that you've made. My list of mistakes didn't stop there, it stopped only once I hit rock bottom and had no choice but to face up to my relationship with money.

As well as looking at what you can learn from the situation, it is also worth exploring why you did things or what your motives were. The root cause of the lack of motivation to deal with financial matters is what you need to try to uncover. For me, this impulsiveness to make a quick return on investment is part of my money persona, and something I've seen repeating time and time again in my life.

Uncovering this pattern and understanding how I sometimes gamble with my financial security has given me the awareness to take a step back, to weigh up the pros and cons, and to structure my finances in a way that lets me take risks but in a more calculated way.

When Kalia looked at her money mistakes, she realised she was always chasing a moving money target, which led her to make rash decisions. When they didn't give her the recognition she craved, her decisions became more rash as she spiralled out of control, until something paid off. This was a cycle that was on repeat throughout her life. Once we uncovered this pattern, Kalia was able to stop letting fear be her driving force and she started to focus her ambitious nature on creating true value in her work, rather than letting it lead her into rash decision making.

Remember your money mistakes. They shine a light on where you need to change focus. This helps you to make the changes necessary to stop making similar mistakes time and time again.

Common Money Mistakes

Money mistakes are not just scenarios from your past where you made some crazy choices or failed to think about the consequences of the decisions you were making. Sometimes, money mistakes are how you deal with the practical elements of managing your money, or the things you fail to manage correctly. Here are some common money mistakes:

Not opening bills. Also include here not paying bills on time, as the two are often linked. Even if you know you are low on funds and might not be able to pay a bill straight away, not opening bills compounds the effect in your mind.

Only making the **minimum payments on credit cards.** It's usually an admission that you've bought something you can't afford.

Using your **credit card for everyday purchases.** This is a problem staring you in the face, the fact that all is not well financially, especially when it is a result of overspending early in the month and then needing to put everyday purchases on your card before your next payday.

Being behind on debt repayments brings a whole host of shame at not being able to meet the minimum requirements of any loans you've taken out.

Falling for scams or **'get rich quick' schemes.** Realising that you've been so daft does leave a bad taste in your mouth. Remember that many intelligent people have fallen for such schemes too.

Spending without thinking. I believe most of us have done this at some point, but some of us are able to make this into an Olympic sport, like we're competing for a medal. When it's small items and you have money, then it doesn't matter so much as it has no adverse effect on your finances. My book addiction on Amazon falls into this category. But there have been instances in the past when I've spent on a whim, on things I truly didn't need and may not have even really wanted, and it's this spending that's a mistake.

Basing **financial decisions on peer pressure.** Keeping up with the Joneses is not a good plan, and if you've done this in the past, then it can be listed in your money mistakes. You now know better though!

Don't know where your money is going. Ever have that feeling that you have no idea where all your money went, and there's still a week or so until payday?

Neglecting to set up a plan for your money. When you're in business, you have a plan, or plan your actions in 90-day or 30-day cycles, but you often neglect making plans for your money.

Never setting money goals. Having a plan is not enough, you need to set goals in order to make sure you achieve what you want. Wondering why you haven't achieved what you wanted when you haven't set goals?

Failing to budget. No one really likes to budget, but not knowing where your money is going, or knowing where it is going but not actually spending it where you want to or need to, is a money mistake that can have an impact on your money mindset.

Quitting your job without a plan. Having an emergency fund to cover your expenses while you're out of work, due to illness or any other situation where you need to leave, would be a great plan. It's what such pots of money are for.

Staying in a dead-end job just because it means you have a wage. Not living your dream, heading in the wrong direction or staying stuck in a job you hate can have an adverse impact on how you think about money.

Not planning for your retirement. This can be considered a money mistake even if you are not approaching retirement yet. Not saving enough for your retirement when you've had the opportunity to do so, and in particular, not joining a scheme where your employer would also contribute (free money!), can lead to regret later in life and impact you just like other money mistakes.

Not refinancing when you should have. Refinancing can help you take control of your finances and reduce your repayments. Not refinancing to a better deal when it's appropriate is nearly as bad where mindset is concerned as refinancing when it's inappropriate. Being appropriate would mean not raising unnecessary additional finance; significant lower payments; reduced interest; or a shorter loan period.

Inadequate insurance. Thinking about taking out life cover or any other insurance is not the same as taking out an insurance policy. While it may not seem like a priority, if you know you should have some insurance to, for example, cover the cost of your funeral or repay your debts on death, then not acquiring this insurance will be a serious money mistake.

Failure to pay yourself first. Saving is important to build an emergency fund so that you feel secure and have enough for the larger things you want in life. Savings should be set to automatic and amount to as much as you can afford, bearing in mind the other components of your spending as per your budget. A good rule of thumb is to build up to savings of ten percent of your income per month.

Failure to review finances on a regular basis. Your relationship with money is like any relationship – it needs constant and careful consideration. You might consider date night once a week or month to help your marriage, so why not pay routine attention to your money?

Based on the list above, you will be able to create a plan for yourself on what actions you need to take to bring your money management up to date. There is a money checklist (MOT) in the resources section at the back of the book which will also help with this.

Jump Off The Treadmill

There is no denying that we live in a consumption driven world. Of course, this brings with it many advantages, but the downside is that it's way too easy to make spending choices that can ultimately haunt you for years. The ad men of the 1950s have evolved and become slicker over time at convincing us that we need things.

How do you survive? You need to pay attention to where you are spending your money, along with developing a healthy dose of scepticism. A dose of common sense thrown in will also help. In other words, you need to develop a 'practical intelligence'. This is a term used by psychologist Karl Albrecht among others. They define this type of intelligence as "the mental ability to cope with the challenges and opportunities of life."

You don't need to be academically minded to have this type of intelligence. It's all about making good judgements in real-life situations. So it doesn't matter if you're like my client Karen, who thought she was no good with maths, and not academically minded.

When I first came across the concept, it was one of those aha moments where I understood exactly why I had made so many spending mistakes. I was the salesman's dream customer, easily convinced that I needed something. I was materialistic without realising it.

By becoming conscious of our spending, we can focus our attention on making better spending decisions. Of course, we don't all see the world in the same way, a concept I think is lost on some people. Have you had a discussion on a topic such as politics? Some people favour the left-wing view while others have more of a right-wing view. Who is correct? Well, that depends on who you ask, but really the answer is neither or both. Most of us live in-between extremes, forming our opinions based on influences from family and our surroundings, particularly the influences we've had in our early years. Our views are shaped by how we see the world, and the fact that someone else views the world differently doesn't make one person wrong and the other right. What seems like a bad purchasing decision to one person might not to someone else.

One thing that a lot of us do have in common though is that we are so immersed in the consumer culture that we act on autopilot. Being on autopilot is not the problem on its own, it's that the view of the world around us is being described by those who profit from it and not by our own world view.

"If we are to change our experience, we must deliberately cultivate new beliefs."
– Laurence Boldt, from *Zen and the Art of Making a Living*.

Conscious spending is your best ally in getting to grips with your money situation. Make sure you are spending in accordance with your view of the world as it is now and how you would like it to be.

Many of us spend a large chunk of time working long hours to earn more money, just to buy more things that we don't always need. It's a treadmill that people just seem unwilling or unable to get off of. You can. I know you can, because I did, and many of the women I work with have done so or are in the process of doing so. It just takes some planning.

If you love the 'buy now pay later' offers, then just remember that these are not always your friend. If your washing machine broke but you don't have the cash this month to buy a new one, then opting for a 'buy now pay later' option might be suitable for you. This is quite different to deciding you'll upgrade your washing machine simply because you don't have to pay for it all in one go.

You might have the option of paying on a credit card, using funds over the next couple of months to pay for the washing machine. While this would attract a small amount of interest, you could have paid it fully in a short space of time.

Which choice is right? I'd say it depends on you. Is paying for things monthly helping you to buy more stuff that you don't need, or to buy them before they are worn out? Or is using a credit card too easy when you just pay the minimum amount? Remember if you do this then the items that you purchase are probably costing you three times as much!

There is no right or wrong answer, so long as you are making your decisions after consciously weighing up all the facts and being sure it is the best decision for you.

All you need to do is think for yourself. Admittedly it's not as easy to do, but just like learning to drive a car, with some practice making sound financial decisions becomes second nature. Frivolous spending habits can soon become a thing of the past.

If you are reading this and thinking that you don't want to deprive yourself, then don't worry, that's not what conscious spending is about. It's a common reaction. I'm telling you that if you stop wasting money on junk and stuff you don't need at this moment in time, then you will be able to gain control over your money quickly and start using it for things that are truly important to you. When you spend money, you are giving up not just the money but also the opportunity to use that money for other things. You can, after all, only spend your money once.

The Savings And Debt Hurdles

Society has conditioned us to think about the here and now and our immediate future. We can have anything we want now, even when we don't have the available cash. There are zero interest deals, terms to pay over extended periods, and the availability of easy-to-reach credit facilities via credit cards and store cards. So why save?

This conditioning has conned many people into believing that they don't need to save. And it is a con!

Do you have an emergency fund? It's essential. Most people don't have a fund to pay for a £400 car repair or to purchase a new washing machine, let alone an emergency fund to cover their expenses should they lose their job or can't keep their business afloat. *The Independent* reported research in 2018 that one in four UK adults have no savings. CNBC in the same year stated that their research showed that one in four Americans had nothing in their emergency fund. These are scary findings.

Resistance to start saving is often a combination of practical money management issues – that is, there is no spare cash – and the mindset that savings aren't necessary.

Often children of parents who were frugal tend to be able to save money more easily when they become adults. This is not always the case though, as our money personality traits also play a role. My parents were frugal and saved regularly for things they needed, yet saving doesn't come naturally to me as my money personality is one that likes to take financial risks rather than create security.

Couple this with unconscious spending habits, and savings are not high on the priority list. This is the biggest lesson I've learned from my story. If I had savings, then the impact of the negative situations that led to my financial downfall would not have been as catastrophic.

Maybe you are like Kerri, a client who always has big ambitions to save but doesn't manage to save enough for her needs, and then feels dispirited so gives up. When you have savings goals, you need to ensure that your budget gives you the allowance you need. Not meeting your savings goals re-enforces the learned behaviour that you are not able to save and misguides you into thinking you are no good with money.

The beauty of learned behaviours is that you can un-learn them. This is a two-part process, one is uncovering how you think about saving, and the other is taking some practical action.

So, if you aren't currently a saver, for reasons other than you don't earn more than your present essential outgoings, which of these ring true for you?

> You do not save because you do not like to have to think about money matters.

> You are more concerned about helping others (people or causes) so that you either use your money to do this instead of saving it, or your charitable actions keep you from earning enough to be able to save.

> You tend to shrug off good money habits, like saving, as you tell yourself you are no good with money.

> Life is to be enjoyed is your motto, and you enjoy spending, so what is the point in saving?

> You spend rather than save, because for you it is more about portraying the wealthy lifestyle than what is in your bank account.

That might have just hurt a little! I didn't set out to write a book about money to be nice to you, but instead have you face up to the reasons you have been thinking about and dealing with money and wealth generation the wrong way.

Once you know the reason you don't save, you can get practical. You don't have to start by saving large sums, putting £10 to £50 per month into a savings plan is a great place to start, particularly if you have debts to repay. To establish the habit of saving, arrange for the transfers from your current to savings accounts to be done automatically. It is also a good habit to 'spend' on your savings goals, before any other spending in the month.

Just as it is easy to not save, it's easy to get into debt, even nowadays, following the financial crash. The stress associated with managing debt, particularly when the amount of debt is significant, coupled with the character assassination that society directs upon those having debt, can soon trap you in a vicious financial cycle. This then leads you to make future financial decisions from a place of fear, scarcity, and panic.

Rewriting this story is concerned with self-love. Your net-worth is not the same as your self-worth. Remember that you are a strong, accomplished and powerful woman. Yes, you are, so don't let your debt obliterate your self-worth. Having debt, despite the negative emotions you probably feel around that fact, does not actually mean that you are no longer accomplished and powerful.

Personally, this was a huge revelation. I thought my financial problems meant that I was no longer accomplished. Sounds a little foolish as I type the words, but my debts seemed to have wiped out all the great accomplishments I had achieved over my working life.

One of the reasons I wanted to work on the book, *Inspirational, Fabulous & Over 40*, was to enable myself to write about my achievements. I'd already spent time journaling about my achievements and knew the power I managed to reclaim, and you can do it too. If you have a blog, why not write about all your achievements? It might inspire someone else, but more importantly it will inspire you. You are inspirational and have achieved great things, you just need to remind yourself of that.

Being in debt does not imply a loss of character. And having no debt does not make you better than anyone else. If we continue to beat ourselves up for having debt, even if it was accumulated for the sake of our education or our business, we will never escape the stress. Do not use your debt as a metric for your self-worth. Instead, take a deep breath. Determine when you feel best. Sleep, eat well, meditate.

You Can Jump High Enough

It is my sincerest wish that you don't ever feel like you can't get past some of the mistakes you've made and the negative or destructive thoughts that you've had about money. It is tough to examine where you've gone wrong, how you have been thinking negatively, and how all of this has got you to where you are now.

No matter how high the hurdles seem in being able to achieve that wealthy mindset, take the action to think abundantly. You can jump high enough and overcome the past. You are worthy of the wealth you desire.

If you choose not to examine the areas that are holding you back, yes, you can become wealthy and you might even get to hold onto that wealth. To increase the odds of this happening, you need to do the work, remove the blocks, become aware of your thoughts and learn from your mistakes.

Reflections:

➢ What would happen if you made rewiring your beliefs your primary focus?

➢ What would happen if you started to take ownership for consciously changing the words that hinder your progress towards financial freedom?

➢ Create a list of all the positive things that have happened because of the money mistakes that you have made or the lessons you can learn from these mistakes.

➢ Create a list of all the positive reasons why creating savings and reducing debt can help you to achieve what you want in life.

Affirmations:

➢ I forgive myself for my past money mistakes.

➢ It is safe for me to pay off all of my debts.

➢ Saving money is natural to me.

➢ I have the power to create all the abundance that I deserve.

"If you put a small value on yourself, rest assured that the world will not raise your price."

ANON

6
You Are Worthy Of Wealth

*T*he complexity of our relationship with money makes it a source of anxiety for many women, particularly when they have not been paying it the attention it deserves. If this is you, here is some great news. It doesn't need to be so complicated. The real key to creating a wealthy lifestyle, whatever that means to you, isn't just about changing how you manage your financial situation, but more about changing how you feel about wealth. This can be done with relative ease if you are willing to put in some effort and face your fears.

Your relationship with money, and ultimately wealth, is no different to any other relationship. It takes love, commitment, patience and understanding. Relationships don't start out being rock-solid. Just ask any couple who have been in a happy relationship for a number of years, and they'll no doubt admit to having to work hard at times and be consistently committed. Their relationship has developed over the years, just as your relationship with money will also develop over time. The earlier you start taking this relationship seriously, the sooner you'll end up happy and wealthy.

Let's be clear though, there is no 'get rich quick' scheme. It's about building the foundations (your mindset) and making them solid.

It's More Than Money

Worthless, that's how I've felt in more than one period in my life. I am sure at some point in your life you too must have felt unworthy to some degree; most women have. Of course, there are some lucky ones who have never felt worthless, but they are in the minority, and if you are not part of this minority, then this is a point worth remembering.

Whether you have felt worthless for just a fleeting moment or for great chunks of your life, it is not your fault. The society that we live in is designed to make us feel worthless, with advertising campaigns that tell us how we should feel, what we should buy and even what we should look like, and a brain that's wired to think negatively when we don't conform to these ideals of the perfect person, family and life.

We are pretty much screwed unless we make the conscious decision to change.

Of course, it is not just our financial situation that can make us feel worthless. I crashed to zero in my twenties, and again in my early forties. I felt worthless not only in my business, but also emotionally as well as financially, all contributing to and magnifying each other, creating a vortex of worthlessness.

I've had a life that many would envy. I graduated with a respectable degree, learned a practical skill and gained a professional qualification, set up my own business in my late twenties, brought home a healthy income, owned nice cars, travelled the world flying business class and even collected some wonderful friends.

The problem was, I just didn't have the emotional stamina to sustain my lifestyle. I take my hat off to those who have similar careers and manage to raise a family. Doing it on your own though, without a reliable long-term partner, is exhausting. I know there are women out there who do it as single parents, but that doesn't mean everyone has the emotional stamina that's needed. I for one didn't, and it left me with an overwhelming feeling of being unworthy.

"No one can make you feel inferior without your consent."

You have probably seen this quote by Eleanor Roosevelt before. I'm unsure in what context she was discussing feeling inferior, of having that feeling of not being good enough, but it is true – no one can make you feel inferior from now on without your consent. How you have felt in the past has been out of your control.

Whether society, family members (especially while growing up), or a current partner has made you feel that you are somehow not worthy of anything, you can draw a line in the sand and decide that you won't let it happen moving forward. Of course, that's easy to write than to do, but you are worthy of everything, including wealth.

If you don't draw that line in the sand, then a catch-22 situation follows. Because you feel unworthy, your ability to maintain or increase your income diminishes, which confirms your feelings of being unworthy, which decreases your ability to accumulate wealth, and so on. This cycle continues until you decide to put your foot on the brakes and change your direction.

I'm Worth It!

Kickstart your 'worthiness' recovery by telling yourself that you are worth it. Unless you believe that you are worthy of the life you want to live, and worthy of receiving the money you need to fund this life, this dream scenario is not likely to happen.

Affirmations like "I am worth it" are great, but they only touch the outer edges of the mindset work needed to think abundantly. It's a good starting point, because you have to start somewhere. If you don't use these affirmations then you should start immediately, and if you already use them then don't stop!

Put down this book for a few minutes, place your hand over your heart, look in the mirror and tell yourself that you are worth it, worth everything you desire. Say it out loud!

At first you are not likely to believe it, but you need to tell this to yourself, every day, several times a day, until you do believe it. Why? Because you are worth it, each one of us is worthy of being wealthy. There is no doubt here, none whatsoever! No matter what events in the past have made you think you are not worthy, or whoever has told you that you are unworthy or useless, this matter is not up for debate. Your worth is indisputable.

I once dated this guy who had recently separated from his wife. We actually co-owned our office building, so it wasn't the wisest of moves right from the start, but that's another story. Anyway, he decided after six months that he was going back to his wife. She liked to control the money and to curtail his love of sports cars. Around the time of our separation, I was looking for a new car with the help of a male friend. I was considering an Audi TT, which was relatively new on the market at the time. This friend helped me realise that I preferred the Porsche Boxter and I was soon settled on this car.

My friend's business partner threw a spanner in the works when he declared, "Oh, that's the girly version of the Porsche 911." Well, I don't do girly, so the hunt was soon switched to finding a Porsche 911, which I did. I got a fabulous silver Porsche with red leather interiors and a suitable private number plate. The first day I drove it to work, I just left it in the car park. I hadn't told anyone the car was mine, but it was obvious from the registration plate.

Half an hour later I got a phone call from my ex, asking if the car was mine. He was quite annoyed that I had purchased the car of his dreams, the one that he wasn't allowed to own. He asked me why I had bought it, to which I simply replied, "I'm worth it," before putting the phone down. That was the moment I discovered just how powerful it is to declare to someone, including myself, that "I am worth it."

Not only did I say the words out loud, but I said them to another person and, more importantly, I truly believed the words. In that moment, there was no doubt.

I encourage you to use affirmations daily, say them to yourself, write them on post-it notes and leave them round your home or office like little love notes to remind yourself how wonderful you are. You can even write them in your journal.

Know You Are Worth It

We are all valuable and can contribute to our family, our community and the world. It's believing in yourself that truly counts. You cannot put a value on yourself until you believe in yourself. Plus, you need to constantly remind yourself of your value so that nothing rocks you – no event, no misguided or nasty words from friends or family.

No one else needs to believe in you, although they will in time, and even if they didn't it wouldn't bother you. Your voice is the only one that counts in matters that affect you. Anyone else's opinion is irrelevant.

To become wealthy, you don't need the kind of belief that Roger Bannister had (I mentioned his story in Chapter 1), as you won't be the first with your background and skills to become wealthy. Instead, be like the others who broke the record in the year after Roger. Believe that what you wish to accomplish is possible by knowing that someone else has achieved what you desire. You can now locate people you want to become your Roger Bannister, follow them on social media platforms and allow them to show you the way forward by reading their blogs or books and, if appropriate, taking their online courses or workshops.

Getting to the place of knowing your true worth is one of life's greatest journeys. It may be a long journey, but it is one that is worth taking. There is not one person out there who cannot go on this journey.

Settling for less than you deserve, chasing love that isn't yours, being afraid to speak authentically and being overly concerned with your partner's, family members' and friends' opinions of you are all signs of not knowing your worth.

I didn't start to really understand my worth until I reached my forties. I got into relationships that were wrong for me, I made a man my priority on more than one occasion and I swallowed my voice in business when I should have spoken. I thought I was living a life on my terms; I was, after all, successful in business and in other areas of my life. It was my relationships (with others, myself, and with my money) that were letting me down and not allowing me to value my worth.

I was only able to know and value my worth after doing the inner work. I had to crash financially and totally burn out emotionally to realise that this was the work that I needed to do. If you only take one thing from this book, I sincerely hope that it is the knowledge that you need to do the inner work to begin to know your true worth.

There are many things you can do to help yourself, as you start to look within. Start by looking at your relationships as they have the greatest impact on how you value your worth. People often say, "Your network is your worth," and while I don't really believe this to be 100 percent true, there is something to be said for surrounding yourself with people who support you and lift you up.

It's worth making the conscious effort to cut out the negative inauthentic people from your life and business and to get to know people who truly share your values. Toxic relationships can plummet your mood quickly and, depending on the relationship, keep you trapped there for quite some time. Often, we cannot ditch these relationships, which is why we persevere with them. You can, however, work on diminishing the impact that they have on you. Spend less time with anyone who does not appreciate you, and counteract the negativity that they leave behind by reconnecting with people who get you and support you.

Start to reconnect with yourself. Kickstart this by taking yourself on a date. You are, after all, in a life-long relationship with yourself, and you need to take the time and energy needed to nurture this relationship. It can be as simple as spending time in your favourite café, reading a book for a couple of hours, going for a long walk, or taking time out for meditating. My girlfriends and I like to take ourselves away for the day to a spa. We each spend time working on ourselves, reading or journaling, but make the time to chat and catch up over lunch. You need to find what works for you, block time out for that in your diary and make yourself a priority, even if it is just for ten minutes. Use what time you can carve out for yourself.

Connecting with nature has wonderful healing properties. My co-author in *The Self-Love Journal: Improve Your Mindset in 90 Days*, Rebecca Norton, is a life coach, and she coaches many of her clients while out walking in nature. Being outdoors around nature helps her clients find balance and focus while they work on the process of looking inwards.

I love to spend time wandering up and down the garden when I need to think things through. In fact, many of the ideas for this book have been forged pacing up and down the lawn at the back of my home. In summers, I even walk barefoot for a true connection to nature. It is cheap therapy and a wonderful way to reconnect with yourself as you anchor yourself to the ground.

Self-Worth Equals Net Worth

It's easy to attach our self-worth to our money issues, but by doing this we unknowingly block the wealth and abundance that is all around us. Money issues are really issues of self-worth; they are within us, rather than in the world around us. Until we feel worthy of money on the inside, we won't feel worthy on the outside (net worth).

Most people with money who have feelings of low self-worth have gained this wealth quickly, such as by winning the lottery or inheriting the wealth, or have longings for the quick wins. Unfortunately, statistics show that such winners often don't keep the money for long. Wishing for a long-lost and wealthy relative to leave you their fortune or a win at the lottery are not financial plans. The way forward is to work on ourselves so that we do feel worthy.

Strive for genuine self-respect that does not depend on others and what they think of you, but what you think of yourself. These thoughts, along with a host of negative beliefs, have been created by our unconscious mind based on things that happened to us in our childhood. We need to untangle these emotions so that any negative feelings about our self-worth do not affect our ability to control our finances.

Is it possible for women to become wealthy in their own right? At this point in history, women are the wealthiest that they have ever been. We hold down top jobs, have our own successful businesses and are becoming the breadwinner in an increasing number of households. According to research in 2018, discussed in *Brides* magazine, 40 percent of households had women as the primary breadwinner. Despite this improvement, women still lag behind men in terms of their earning power. If you listen to the news, you will have heard stories of women not earning the same as men for the same job, which is crazy all these years after the Equal Pay Act. It's the same across the world, not just here in the UK.

We also have less when it comes to savings, particularly in terms of retirement funds. According to research by *Aegon*, men in the UK have an average pension pot of £73,600, and for women, this figure is only £24,900. This is crazy when women, on average, live for longer! We need to do something about this, and make sure we're adequately covered financially for a long retirement.

If we work on being worthy, then perhaps we can make the leap to becoming equal to men in the wealth stakes.

Net worth is a measure of your financial situation, and it's one of the most useful yet often underused measures. The purpose of calculating your net worth is for you to ascertain, in a numerical form, where you are now. The formula is quite simple:

Total value of all your assets minus the total value of all your liabilities.

In other words, it is what you've got left. That's it.

Every financial move you make from now should be aimed at increasing your net worth. You can increase your net worth by either increasing your assets or reducing your liabilities.

It is possible that your net worth is a negative figure, if you owe more than you own. It is quite common for young people who are just starting out to have a

---

negative net worth, as they often carry substantial amounts of student loan debt, credit card debt and personal loans but have not yet had the chance to acquire many assets. If you do have negative net worth, then your first goal will be to increase your net worth to zero as soon as possible.

Assets are the things that you own, which will either retain their value or have the potential to increase in value, although it is possible for them to also fall in value.

Write a list of all the items that you own with their value. Don't include vehicles because they don't retain value and they certainly don't go up in value unless you own a classic car. Also don't list all the electronics and gadgets that you own within your home and office, because again they're going to go down in value. You can include the following physical and financial assets:

Land and property

Family heirlooms and antiques (because they're going to retain value)

Bank accounts (not your current account, just include savings and investment accounts)

Stocks and shares

Corporate and government bonds

Retirement fund (pension scheme)

Liabilities are the opposite of assets and are the value of what you owe. The types of liabilities that you may have could include the Bank of Mum and Dad (or even Bank of Husband/Wife if you run your finances separately), loans from family members, personal loans, as well as other financial commitments. Other liabilities can be:

Credit card balances

Car finance (If you have taken a loan out to purchase a vehicle, then it is like having a personal loan, even if it's secured on the actual car)

The scary part, for some, is adding up the total debt. It can be a real wakeup call that you need to act and get your finances in order.

You Are Not Cinderella

"When we feel that we aren't good enough, we also fear that we will never have enough."

I totally agree with this quote by Nancy Levin. Unfortunately, this belief becomes a self-fulfilling prophecy, and our unconscious mind makes sure we never have enough.

The challenge for each of us is to become our own Prince Charming and take back control of our finances. So many women are willing to hand over control to someone else, whether that's a husband, partner or even a professional advisor such as an accountant.

I see friends staying in marriages for financial security, and it breaks my heart knowing they could become so much more if they would just allow themselves to spread their wings and fly. It's not about leaving their husbands and getting divorces; their marriages could be different if they had the courage to work on their self-worth and then start to become financially independent. Changing the dynamics around wealth within the relationship with a partner can have a huge impact on the rest of the relationship. That's where it becomes even scarier and keeps them stuck in the role of Cinderella.

I always wanted to be financially independent, something I adopted from a young age. The only person I have ever had to rely on was my father. Luckily for me, he's a pretty old-fashioned guy and as an unmarried daughter, I've remained his 'responsibility' as he sees it. It's had its share of problems, but overall, I have remained responsible for my financial position all my life. It brings with it a sense of freedom. There is an army of single women out there who'll get this. The longer you remain financially independent, the harder it becomes to hand over control, especially when you take time to learn the basics.

I, without a doubt, would not have made the financial mistakes that I did, if I had handed over the purse strings to someone else. That scenario may have resulted in me becoming very wealthy and staying that way, but it could equally have left me worse off financially. Either way the control over my destiny would not have been mine, and to feel truly worthy of wealth, control is essential.

Being in charge of the purse strings allows you to make the mistakes, then learn from them.

Even if you are not the breadwinner in the family, you can still become your own Prince Charming. I encourage any woman, or man, who isn't making any money outside of the home, to talk to their spouse about being compensated for the work they do looking after the children and the home. This will improve their self-worth and allow them to make financial decisions for themselves, such as saving for a rainy day or for retirement.

Whenever we have conversations about money, what we're really talking about is control. If one person has all the money in a relationship, they take control over the other partner, whether done intentionally or not. A relationship doesn't have to be about an absolute 50:50 split of power, but it does have to be equal when it comes to the feeling of control.

It's not always the partner with the wealth who pulls the purse strings. My first partner, who I met at university, had his purse strings controlled by his parents as it was family money. They were lovely people, but I can only imagine what it would have been like had we stayed together. It wasn't something he could live with either, and he moved to the USA to break the link and take control. It seemed extreme at the time, but now I understand how important it is to have this control.

Small Steps

Your potential is intangible and a lot of it comes down to your mindset. If you develop an abundance mindset (I'm sharing my insights into this throughout the book), then you will sharpen your mind and develop the abundant and wealthy future you deserve.

Small steps can lead to big decisions, you just need to take the first step to getting started.

It's not about where you are now, it is about where you are heading and how you are going to get there. It's time to stop ignoring your potential. You are a powerful and wealthy woman and you need to remember that money flows to those who value themselves!

Reflections:

- ➤ Do you feel worthy of the level of wealth you desire? If not, do you know why?
- ➤ What do you need to believe about yourself before you can achieve your dreams?
- ➤ What relationships do you have that have a positive impact on your ability to increase your worth? Think in terms of self-worth and your net worth.
- ➤ What relationships have a negative impact on your ability to increase your worth, and how are they affecting you?
- ➤ What conversations are you avoiding having, either with yourself or with someone else?

Affirmations:

- ➤ I can do this, I am worth it, I deserve to be happy and wealthy.
- ➤ I am powerful, confident, and capable of fulfilling all my dreams.
- ➤ I believe in myself!
- ➤ I am worthy.

"Bad habits are like chains that are too light to feel until they are too heavy to carry."

Warren Buffett

7

Remove The Elastic Band

*I*t makes me want to cry, every time I see a photo of an elephant or donkey just standing there, looking like they have been mistreated or shackled. You've probably seen the photos I'm referring to being shared on social media, where animals are bound with rope or chains to a plastic chair or to nothing at all. It is heart-breaking to see that they have been conditioned to accept this ill treatment and to remain stuck where they are, despite their reality being the opposite.

Some of us are like those animals, chained to our beliefs, our old ways, unable to move forward. However, unlike those animals, we have somewhere else we can go to, we can escape. We only need to realise that we either aren't really tied to anything, or it's something that isn't strong enough to keep us stuck. This belief, coupled with courage, can propel us in the direction of our idea of financial freedom.

These beliefs act like elastic bands – they keep snapping us back to the old ways, the ways that keep us stuck, while all the time convincing us that this is where we are meant to be. So how do we get rid of these bands? Well, one way, though not recommended, is to stretch them, making ourselves more and more uncomfortable, until they snap and are no longer a problem. The other better way is to remove the bands, or at the very least loosen their elasticity, so that they don't keep snapping us back to our 'normal' and away from the wealth we desire.

These elastic bands, while there as a protection mechanism in our unconscious, can be troublesome.

Money Stories

There are two sides to mastering your money. On one side is practical money management, on the other are emotions. These sides don't have equal weight. It's the emotional side that plays the most significant role in determining whether your relationship with money will run smoothly or be turbulent. This relationship is summarised in your money story.

Every person has a story to tell, and like all stories there are numerous plots and sub-plots as well as good and bad storylines. Your money story has all the same attributes and is a combination of several money stories.

Here are some common money beliefs that provide the synopsis for many money stories. See how many you can relate to:

- ➢ Money is evil
- ➢ I don't deserve to be wealthy
- ➢ I should not earn more money than my parents

- I should not earn more money than my spouse
- Most rich people got their money illegally or don't deserve it
- Spending money on myself is selfish
- It is not spiritual to earn lots of money
- If I am rich, then my friends won't like me anymore
- I must work extremely hard to make lots of money
- I'm not good enough

You will no doubt be able to produce your own list and I encourage you to do so. You might get a few surprises in there.

These background beliefs create negative cycles, which we are often not aware of in our day-to-day activities, because they are in our unconscious. These can be termed as limiting beliefs or money blocks, because not only do they not serve us but they also limit our thinking to varying degrees.

Some of your issues might be quite near the surface and hence easy to identify, but we all have money stories currently affecting us that are buried much deeper. You learn a lot of the plots of your story from the people who've played a significant role in your upbringing. In fact, the main plots for this money story are developed before the age of seven.

This totally blew my mind – no wonder I had been terrible with money! I was letting the junior version of me control my decision making as an adult. Do you know any seven-year-olds? Would you trust them to consistently make rational decisions?

Where did we get the information to develop these stories? They are based on several things: How you observed others close to you earn their money, spend it, or save it – if indeed any money was saved. This is not just what you saw, but what you may have heard both directly and indirectly. Even the seemingly harmless comments, like "money doesn't grow on trees" or "we're not made of money," can have quite a profound effect on you at such a young age.

Our unconscious mind takes these beliefs and reinforces them by playing them out time and time again. By the time we are well and truly into adulthood, we have created a complicated money story that is personal to us and one that we believe whole-heartedly to be true.

There will, of course, be people who attract money into their lives even with unhelpful, and indeed harmful, money stories, but they don't keep hold of their money as these beliefs will take hold of their actions, so that they soon lose/ spend all their money.

There are stories of people who have won the lottery and become millionaires, only to be back where they started a few years later and, in some cases, they've even had to file for bankruptcy. Lottery winners are given help with investments by having access to financial advisors, but what they need is access to someone who can help them get their head around having so much money.

Becoming aware of your money stories so that you can stop them tripping you up when you are creating wealth is an important step. You should not put this off or wait until you achieve a certain level of wealth.

As with a lot of work around mindset, awareness is an important and vital step, making it worthwhile to take a step back and give yourself time to reflect on those thoughts that are running in the background and hindering you from achieving financial freedom.

Rewriting History

There is good news, even for those with money stories that belong in the horror section. You can lightly edit your money stories where necessary or even entirely rewrite them. You are the author and editor of this story, so all is not lost.

The first step is to find the stories that are holding you back. Many do not get far with this, as it can take some time. All money mindset work consists of taking small steps, consistently, over a period of time. If you aren't willing to devote the time, then there isn't much point in reading books like this. If you are serious, then don't skip this step (or any of the other steps!). It is not a step that should be missed, as it is vital for revealing a clear picture of what negative beliefs you have dragged from the past into your current situation around money. If you then rewrite these beliefs into a positive story, then these stories will no longer hinder you from obtaining the wealth that you desire.

My money mentor, Kendall Summerhawk, identified that there are four dangerous money mindsets:

 ➢ I love what I do, but it's not about the money.
 ➢ If I want to make more, I'll have to work harder.
 ➢ I don't think I can make more than I did when I had a job. (Sometimes, this can show up as – I don't think I can make more than my spouse / partner / parent.)
 ➢ I don't think I can handle it if I get bigger (in business).

If you examine this list and the list of money beliefs in the previous section, you'll see that you are not alone in your thinking. Many of us are walking around with similar beliefs.

Our stories might be different but the beliefs that we've developed are common. This is because Society has played a huge part in the development of our money stories. Our culture and the media contribute in creating a fear-based story that is tempting to buy into. I grew up in the UK at a time when I only had three TV channels, yet the youth of today have hundreds of TV channels, the internet and social media all perpetuating this fear-based culture. They are bombarded from all sides. It's not just the younger members of society who're plagued by this narrative, I see plenty of people in their forties and older who are falling for all the media bombardment of doom and gloom.

The best way to help yourself rewire your brain is to unplug from the matrix as much as possible. I say as much as possible because sometimes, especially when you are in business, you need to stay plugged in. But distancing yourself from the matrix can help you become more centred on what is happening to you and happening directly around you.

If you don't believe me, listen to the news or look at a newspaper and see what the headlines are today. How many are doom and gloom? Is the stock market about to crash, at the lowest levels since so-and-so year, is there a fear of a recession? You'll find the word fear, or a suggestion of a potential fear, in a lot of the articles about the economy. This will be the same if you are in the UK, mainland Europe, United States, Canada or Australia, or anywhere else in the modern world.

Know what happens next? Herd mentality plays a part, and fear spreads across social media, and then the markets react to the fear of the people. The news story has been justified as our fears are coming real.

It's the same with society's view of money and those with money. You can work out what your views about money are by mediating on and writing in your journal the answers to the following questions. Think of those pivotal moments in your childhood that were centred around money and finances.

What is your earliest money memory?

What did your parents say about money?

What did your parents tell you directly about money?

Note down anything that you or your parents did or did not do around money. This is very important.

Rewriting your money story is an ongoing process that you can refer to each time you think of another money memory or are ready to improve your story to the next level. You might be quite surprised with the number of stories that come back to you once you start clearing your first set of limiting beliefs. It's a bit like peeling an onion – you peel back one layer, to find another and then another. You might also shed a tear or two during this process.

You might already know of some examples of how you have sabotaged yourself regarding money and wealth. It's time to write in your journal again, and answer these questions:

* What does money mean to you today?
* How does money make you feel?
* Do you believe that money is good or bad?
* What has been the theme in your life for the past few years?
* Do you think that you are good with money?
* Do you believe that you deserve to spend money on yourself?
* What do you fear most about not having enough money or having excess money?

Predominant Wealth Theme

Has there been a set of stories with a similar theme prominent in your childhood, showing up time and time again in your adult life?

You will have one, or maybe two, predominant money stories. These are the money stories that have the most influence over your relationship with money, and many of your other money stories will stem from this predominant story.

Once you have collected a selection of money stories from your journaling, you will be able to categorise them based on similar themes. Once you have these themes, spend some time exploring if these themes can be traced back to one predominant story.

"My family aren't wealthy, therefore I'm not." Iris, like many of the other women I coach, was a first-generation high-income earner. She was the first in her family to go to university, and the first to earn six-figures annually. For some women, the experience of having money is so unfamiliar and daunting that they often become overwhelmed. While she loved her parents, she didn't want to be like them in terms of wealth, yet despite this she was constantly being pulled backwards by the belief that because she didn't come from a wealthy family, she could not become wealthy. Managing money became a burden for her, and any extra income she generated was lost through bad investments or frivolous spending that seemed to be out of control, and in fact she was often spending far more than she earned.

Iris, like many women, whether they grew up in poverty or not, did not have a successful model for how to make, maintain, and invest her money. By operating out of fear of her finances, she often failed to see the opportunities to build wealth. Her decision making was also keeping her in the same cycle as her parents.

For Iris, this money story evolved round the relationship that her mother had with her siblings. She had seen her mother talk to her grandmother and aunts about the woman who married her brother, describing this woman as having ideas of grandeur and always wanting the best of everything and thinking she was better than them. Every time Iris's dad was promoted at work, her mum wanted to keep it quiet from her family and not show that they had wealth. It was a message that young Iris received loud and clear.

Are you a little bit like Iris? Maybe your predominant money story is different, but it's led you to the belief that stepping outside of the family's wealth parameters isn't a wise choice, or that having money won't allow you to fit into your current social circle. The result of such beliefs is a fear of dealing with or having money.

If so, one way forward is to identify your worst fear around money and ask yourself, "What is the worst that can happen?"

I'm not next to you as you read this, but if I were, I wouldn't be surprised to see resistance and maybe a few tears. I'm asking you now, "What is the worst that can happen?"

Often, the fear of being a bag lady or living on the street is looming in our head and seems much more likely than it actually is. Despite financial ruin I never had to live on the streets, which just goes to show that when the worst happens, the worst actually hasn't happened.

What would happen if you lost your job or were suddenly unable to continue operating in your current business? What would you do next? Who could you turn to for help? How long will it take you to get back on your feet? What we often don't realise is that we possess more inner and outer resources than we think.

"Put your oxygen mask on first!" This is the title we put on Tina's predominant money story. She was always taking care of others first, so much so that her financial goals were constantly on hold.

She was a classic nurturer personality who was always looking out for someone else, whether it was her parents, her younger sibling, her partner, her partner's family and even her clients. Caring and compassion were high on her values list. They are good values to have.

On the surface, it doesn't seem wrong to be a nurturer, but the problem is that some women take on the nurturing role too much and forget to put their own oxygen mask on. Tina wasn't focused on the profit her business made, and as a result her income potential and future savings suffered. She wanted to grow her business, yet helping people was constantly being put in front of making profits. The result was a lack of financial security, limited savings and investments, and high anxiety around her financial future.

If you can relate to Tina's money story, then you should consider what putting your own oxygen mask on first looks like.

Identifying and starting to heal the relationship issues caused by your predominant money story will have the greatest impact in the shortest amount of time.

Start Afresh

Choice. We all have a choice when it comes to how we think about anything, from money and wealth to love, to what foods we like to eat.

Can we start afresh and create a new money story from scratch? A new one that we would like to live by rather than the old ways? I wish I could wave a magic wand and say yes, but it's not that easy.

You can change your beliefs when it comes to dealing with money and all things financial. To do this, you will need to deconstruct your money story. Remember that your money story was developed over a considerable amount of time, and the older you are, the more the story and all its component parts will have been reinforced many times over.

Deconstructing your money stories can in itself take years if you are doing this by yourself, which of course you can. You don't have to invest in a coach, although this will speed up the process.

Don't be put off by the length of time it takes. You will start to see improvements from the moment you start taking this deconstruction work seriously.

Admission time: I worked on deconstructing my money story for just over five years, not always at full throttle, but during that time, I went from being in debt with a modest salary to earning five-figures each month while working part-time and having no debt. It's very much like life itself, a journey.

The big question each of my coaching clients have asked is: how do you start to deconstruct your money story?

Think about each of your memories that have led to a limiting belief and then think about what else it could mean. What are the opposite facts? Keep asking yourself this, until you have at least half a dozen other possible conclusions for each memory.

Remember, this is your story, so you get to choose how it is written.

When you have rewritten your story, don't stop there. Look at what the old story had prevented you from doing. Now is the time to write an action plan to correct your course, so that you can follow your new story.

As you practise writing your money story, you will notice that you begin to become more aware of when old money stories come into play. Paying attention to your thoughts will make you more aware of what you are thinking about and how those thoughts are affecting your current situation.

Old money stories might keep reappearing. Your unconscious mind believes that these stories are true, and it will take time to reprogram your unconscious mind to accept your new version of the stories as the truth. When you think of those old stories, tell yourself that is what they are – just an old story that you have, in fact, replaced with a new one.

One way to help would be to record your new story in your voice. Most modern phones have a recording option. Once you've recorded it, listen to it daily and start to feel yourself opening up to the new possibilities that your new story is going to bring.

To rewrite your money story, you need to identify those money stories from your past that hold limiting beliefs and blocks. These can be beliefs that you picked up from your family when you were a child, or beliefs that formed from the mistakes you have made in your adult life.

By writing these stories down and examining them, you'll probably find that the mistakes you've made in your adult life can be traced back to limiting beliefs that you first picked up as a child.

Then you need to reword what you think the story meant. Try thinking of the opposite scenario to your negative belief. Finally, you need to keep reminding yourself of the new money story.

The unearthing of these money stories is an ongoing process, so don't think of a couple and assume you are done. Try not to work with more than five beliefs/stories when you first start the process. Dealing with the emotions around some of your limiting beliefs can be quite draining at times. You need to give yourself time to process these emotions.

Once you've dealt with the old stories and turned them around, you can devote some time to creating an entirely new script.

Dress Rehearsal

To help you write your new money stories and create the mindset that will allow you to attract the wealth you desire, you need to rehearse the new stories and the new life you will live.

To create your future, you must rehearse it. Our minds learn a lot through repetition. Maybe not having to write 'lines' in detention as a young child, but we have generally spent our lives learning by repetition. Once our mind has learned something, then it becomes second nature and we act on automatic pilot.

Think about when you learned to drive a car. I certainly had my doubts when I was learning to drive that I wouldn't be able to find driving an easy task, as there was so much to think about, but with the repetition of driving, the act becomes almost automatic and can be done without thinking about changing the gear or looking in your rearview mirror. Heck,

I can now get to places without knowing how I got there, everything is so automatic.

Whether you repeatedly do a task consciously or unconsciously, your mind picks up on the fact that you are carrying out the task repeatedly, so it makes the assumption that you want to learn the task.

We need to repeat our new ways in our mind, and keep repeating them long enough for our mind to notice and get them, and then the new ways will become part of who we are.

The change that will result from these rehearsals will often take time to come to fruition. Most of us have years and years of negative beliefs to work through, but it's a journey that is worth taking.

Create a movie of how your life is to be, in as much detail as possible, making sure it's filmed in technicolour with surround sound.

If you struggle in creating a movie, start with a single image and build from there, one scene at a time. Explore the images from an emotional viewpoint. How do you feel about your ideal life of financial freedom? What emotions come up as you explore these thoughts?

Have a little faith too. You need to trust that you already have this. This vision is yours, in all its completeness, from start to finish, so it is up to you how it all plays out. Remember, you are the producer, director, script writer and lead actor.

When you are happy with your 'movie', you can play it in your mind like a dress rehearsal for what is to come. The key to this process lies in the practice of it. Revisiting your visualisation, your movie, is how you're going to best succeed. Play this movie in your mind every morning and evening, and any time that you need to during the day.

This exercise is a great way to remind yourself of what is important to you. Your unconscious mind can work on helping you move towards this vision for the future, even when you are asleep or carrying out daily routine tasks.

"Make a choice, you just decide, what it's gonna be, who you're gonna be, how you're gonna do it. Just decide, and then from this point, the Universe is gonna get out your way."

~ Will Smith

Final Thoughts ...

How our parents or guardians handled their money is quite often how we end up managing our money. Not only can we look at our early memories and identify those money stories recurring throughout our adult life, we can also look at the stories that played out in our parents' and even grandparents' lives. The more family history we have access to, the more we can examine how it has influenced us in how we think about money.

Just as you've developed your relationship with money from what you learned from your parents, your children will learn from you. Changing your money story to one that is positive has the added benefit of boosting your children's chances of financial success.

Reflections:

> What did your trip down memory lane by looking at your money stories reveal to you about your wealth patterns?

> What predominant stories (frameworks) have you adopted from people in your life? Even though they were well intentioned, which ones are you now ready to reframe and release?

> What money stories do you currently have playing out in your life? How would your life change if you changed these money stories?

> What money stories would you like your children or grandchildren to learn from you (either now or in the future)?

Affirmations:

> I give myself permission to feel good about money.

> Money creates a positive impact on my life.

> Success and wealth define my way of life.

> I always think in wealthy ways.

"In life we do not attract what we want, we attract who we are."

MOFFAT MACHINGURA

8
Walking Through Fire

*I*n early 2016, my friend Julie sent me a link to a website, stating excitedly that she had booked this company for our business gala scheduled for International Women's Day. The website claimed that "a fire walk is the most inspirational journey you will probably undertake." It soon dawned on me that this was something I was going to have to do – as one of the organisers, it seemed like I had little choice in the matter.

The thought of walking barefoot over hot glowing embers filled me with fear, but I knew I would have to face this fear. The pre-walk talk that they give, while the wood is being set alight, covers the physics of how it is possible to walk over the smouldering embers, but even facing the 'facts' – which did seem plausible even to someone like me who was never good at science – did very little to dispel the fear. Logic never seems to dispel fear, not in the short term anyway.

There is a reason why this is, for many people, a truly inspirational journey. Once you've done the seemingly impossible walk, your mindset shifts. This shift was not immediate, but I was aware that I had faced my fear and gone against my instincts that walking over glowing embers was going to hurt. It is a catalyst though, and later that month I handed in my notice at the 'day job' totally out of the blue, a decision that seemed right for me at that time. I just knew that I was ready to take the leap of faith and go headfirst into full-time self-employment again.

If you get the chance to do a fire-walk, take it. Give yourself the chance to exhale the fear.

Exhale The Fear

Fear is a natural and powerful emotion. Sometimes we feel it in ways that are unwarranted or at a level that's inappropriate. Even though the feelings it generates inside us are annoying, they are a wakeup call that we have issues that we need to address.

This fear can be broken down into two main categories:

- ➢ We are not going to get something that we want
- ➢ We will lose something we already have

When it comes to wealth and money, this fear can be very intense. Some people can actually have a fear of money or spending it. This intense fear is called Chrometophobia or Chremtophobia (it's even got two names, it's that scary!).

Even without this intense fear of money itself, fear shows up for many of us in relation to our wealth. We fear that we are not going to get the wealth we desire, not going to live the life of our dreams, not going to achieve financial freedom or the success we desire in our business or career. The fear extends beyond pure money-related matters.

This fear creates an imprisoning pattern that keeps us stuck. Stuck in jobs and relationships, living with situations that are not supporting our highest good and our future wealthy selves. No matter in what ways we are disconnected in our lives, this disconnectedness is a perceived feeling that covers the more deeply seated emotion of fear. Fear that is unwarranted or inappropriate and not what the emotion was designed to do – protect us.

It dominates us, even when we aren't aware of its presence. To make matters worse, this fear often becomes the prime motivator for our financial decision making. It's therefore imperative that we learn to become aware of fear and start to heal the root cause of fear.

Sometimes though, we do succumb to fear, and if we do then we need to forgive ourselves. It's perfectly natural for the fear to become so intense that it temporarily paralyses us. This has happened to many a great person.

I've always been impressed with the great English actor Stephen Fry. Back in the mid-nineties, he was several performances into the West End run of a play when he disappeared. It's reported that his home phone's message said, "I'm sorry. I'm so very sorry." It was later discovered that Fry, who is bipolar, had succumbed to stage fright. In fact, stage fright is quite common among actors, despite it being their preferred profession. They learn to embrace this fear but sometimes, in spite of this, it gets the better of them.

When it comes to money, we can learn to deal with it emotionally and practically, but fear can still get a grip on our financial decision making. Stephen Fry is still a great actor and he's still hired as an actor; it would be a shame if he never again acted because of this one time he let the fear take control. Yet when it comes to our wealth, many of us let fear take control and paralyse us. We can acknowledge that this may happen from time to time, but we do have the choice to not let this paralysis be for life.

When we recognise we are acting in fear, we can acknowledge this perceived disconnection and make a choice to live another way where we embrace the fear and use it to propel us to greater things.

Our behaviours then shift from being motivated by fear to being motivated by love. We still may have moments of fear, but its power over us lessens as we continue down the path.

There are several ways that you can start to embrace the fear:

➢ Accept that you may need to take some risks when making decisions in relation to your finances and how you intend to create your wealth.

➢ Do not allow procrastination and lethargy over dealing with financial matters keep you stuck in the mud. Money may not be your prime motivator, and

> you may have no interest in dealing with it on a day-to-day basis, but it is an important part of life that should not be ignored.

> Start to become more open about money and start talking about it. Talk about it with your coaches and mentors and also your partner and family.

> Stop avoiding the truth when it comes to understanding your current financial position.

Avoiding The Truth

Avoiding the truth about your financial situation is a popular club to belong to, but just because it has so many members doesn't mean you should want to be one of them. We tend to avoid the truth about our finances for a whole host of reasons. Tucked away behind these reasons, out of sight, is typically the emotion of fear.

When it comes to our financial situation, we are fearful of:

> Learning to understand the basics.

> Becoming successful and one of those rich people that aren't very nice.

> Not knowing how we would handle success in our business.

> Out-earning our friends and family.

Do you have these fears? Take a few minutes to reflect on what other fears you have around money, finances and being wealthy.

Facing up to these fears, just by becoming aware that they exist and are affecting how you consciously feel about money and how you deal with your finances on a day-to-day basis, is enough to take that leap of faith to start to overcome the barriers that are stopping you from achieving financial freedom.

I regularly talk to women who are afraid of opening their credit card statements, checking their bank balances regularly or creating a budget.

For some this fear shows up as anxiety, for some others it's stress, and for the lucky ones it is just a minor irritation. Fear can trigger severe physical symptoms in the body or in the mind, even when it has nothing to do with the actual state of our finances. You can have anxiety over money when you're struggling to make ends meet or even when you're a successful businesswoman needing to stay on top of her game and keep earning six-figures. However it shows up in your life, it needs dealing with.

If you are unsure whether you are suffering from financial anxiety, then please take a moment to consider the following questions. If you answer 'yes' to any of these questions, chances are that you are suffering from some level of financial anxiety:

- ➢ When you think about the subject of money, do you experience overwhelm, panic or confusion on any level of severity?
- ➢ Do you have concerns about your job security and/ or your future business income levels?

> ➤ Do you have sleepless nights, worrying about how you might pay your bills or how you'll manage your finances in the future?

The most important quality you need in order to change your wealth, and in fact the entire course of your life, is courage. The courage to face your fears and walk through them. There's no point in sugar coating this, you'll need bucket loads of courage. You need courage to live in poverty and you need courage to live a life of wealth. I know where I want to direct my courage towards. Where do you want yours to be directed?

To help you develop that courage, here are some practical tips that can help you get yourself organised and alleviate some of your worries:

Begin by decluttering your financial paperwork. No fancy filing system or expensive cabinet is needed. You can regain control by implementing just a few simple steps. Start by throwing away anything that's no longer relevant. You don't need the last gas bill from your previous home of four years ago!

It's a great feeling to rip up, shred or burn unwanted paperwork. Enjoy the process!

Categorise any letters or paperwork and file them away in a labelled drawer or box. It is good practice to implement your filing in date order.

Make sure that you open all letters as soon as they arrive. A 'deal with later' pile is not a good idea, as later never arrives.

If any correspondence requires immediate attention, then simply take the necessary action. Five minutes of anguish dealing with it now is healthier than having it hang out and fester in your mind for weeks.

Set a weekly date to manage your paperwork. This might include simple tasks such as filing away paperwork or paying your latest bills.

Create a simple budget. Calculate what you can sensibly afford to spend each week/month on all the main categories of expenditure such as rent/mortgage, food, car, kid's activities, etc. When you have set the budget, adhere to it as much as you can. Each payday, examine the budget and remind yourself how you plan to spend your money.

It is good practice to set yourself some financial goals. This might include paying off a certain amount of debt in the next six months or saving up a set amount by a certain date. Write these financial objectives down and review them at least once weekly.

Not dealing with the fundamental basics of money management lets the fear creep into your mindset, thus increasing your risk of making the wrong or misguided decisions about your wealth.

Risky Business

Dealing with money and creating wealth is a risky business. One of the best ways to reduce this risk, and ultimately your fear, is by becoming aware of your financial situation. As management thinker Peter Drucker is often quoted as saying, "you can't manage what you don't measure." It's the same with managing your money. You need to be aware of your money situation, from what you are spending money on, to how much you are saving, to the level of debt you are servicing.

Some popular but crazy ways of dealing with this risk are:

- ➢ Abdicate responsibility
- ➢ Do nothing, and bury your head in the sand until you have no choice but to act
- ➢ Procrastinate – why do today what you can put off again and again?
- ➢ Mix of the above

I see at least one of these strategies being used by all my clients, even the ones that are already successful and are just honing their money skills. Even when I had my money story turned around and was back to earning good money with no debt, I could still relate to one or two of these strategies in certain areas of my finances. None of us are perfect all the time.

Let's look at the risks of each of these strategies.

Your money is far too important to abdicate responsibility for it to someone else. If your business so requires, you can hire a bookkeeper or accountant or even use the services of a financial advisor to guide you through the marketplace of personal finance options to select a pension fund / Superannuation.

However, you cannot and should not delegate the responsibility of your finances to someone else. You need to take ownership. Let's face it, who else is invested as much in your financial success as you are? No one, no matter how much they are being paid to assist you.

Ask questions, try to understand the basics, read the literature, and take an interest in what is happening with your finances, wealth and business profits. Your accountant and financial advisor will not think you as a nuisance or a problem client for this; they are more likely to count you as one of their favourite clients. As an ex-accountant and financial advisor, let me tell you there is nothing more soul-destroying then spending time sorting out someone's finances for them to have no interest in the work you've done or the improvements you've made or the opinions you've shared.

The do-nothing strategy is born out of a paralysing fear of dealing with your finances. It's one of the riskiest money strategies as it is so easy to succumb to this fear. If I started walking across a motorway bridge, then by the time I got to the middle I'd be feeling pretty much like I couldn't put one foot in front of the other. This might not seem rational or a big deal to you, but it is for me. I've been there, frozen in my tracks, stuck in the middle of the bridge, in the worst place I could possibly want to be.

Not having the option to ignore the situation, I needed to push through, dig deep and get the courage to carry on and get to safety. The problem when it comes to financial fear is that being in the middle of the bridge somehow doesn't seem that bad, so we decide to stay put instead of pushing through. Camping there might not allow us to be where we want to be – in the five-star hotel a few hundred yards away from the edge of the bridge – but we're okay for now.

The third strategy is procrastination. Often, we adopt this strategy because we are too busy, the kids need to be taken to their next dance class, the dog needs walking, we can't find our calculator, or we're just too tired after a day in the office. Or, it's a way to think you are getting out of the do-nothing strategy, just that you are delaying the action.

Whatever the reason for adopting this strategy, every time you procrastinate out of fear, every time you avoid acting to take care of your finances, you are unconsciously sending a message to yourself that, "I am not worth the effort." Which in turn starts a self-perpetuating cycle.

There are, however, things that you can start to do to reduce risk and stop the procrastination cycle. Take a good look at all the areas of your finances and acknowledge what you need to do to bring these areas into good standing.

Look at how much money you allocate in the prime areas of housing, debt repayment, food, savings and discretionary spending (everything else!). Are you up to date with your debt repayments? Have you reviewed your retirement plans recently? Is your income stable? Can you generate more?

See the resources section at the back of the book to give yourself a financial MOT or speak to a financial coach for accountability.

When you have your list, break each point down into actionable steps, which will only take a short amount of time. Then whenever you have a spare fifteen or thirty minutes, you can look at this list, choose an item and hey presto, in thirty minutes or less you will have something to cross off your list.

Procrastination Costs

Some costs of not dealing with your finances are short term and may only be small monetary amounts, but these small amounts add up.

Switching telephone contracts seems easy enough, but what about when you don't find time to go online or to the store to look for a new contract because you don't really want a new phone? This was the situation my client Emily found herself in. When she jumped on a call with me, her mobile phone contract had ended three months earlier. Because she had not explored her options, the phone provider was still charging her the same rate as during the 24-month contract, even though the original charge had been worked out to include payment for the physical phone.

It took her literally ten minutes to look at options online and sign up to a 12-month contract for calls and data only, saving her around £30 per month. The last three months had cost her £90, which may not seem much but when you have credit card debt, it's like being slapped in the face twice because using this money against the balance could have saved her interest payments as well.

Auto renew functions on subscriptions are great for not forgetting to renew, but when you no longer want to subscribe and aren't vigilant with dealing with your finances, not cancelling in time can be costly.

Some costs have longer-term effects on your finances, and unless you start to address them as soon as possible, the impact will become more profound.

Paying the minimum on your credit card bill is a prime example. This should only be done if you are in absolute dire straits and cannot manage to repay any more as the rest of your money is needed for basic food and shelter.

If you are unsure if you will always be able to afford the full balance of your credit card, it makes perfect sense to set up your auto payment to just cover the minimum amount. If you miss the deadline to pay more of the balance, then you end up paying interest, and if you forget next month as well, you will be paying interest on interest. You could easily end up paying off this debt over several more years then necessary than if you had just taken the situation in hand.

Not building an emergency savings fund is another pitfall. Starting to save is key. It doesn't have to be much, you just need to get around to starting. Gimmicks and savings games seem to help here. The kind of games you play where you save £1 in the first week, £2 in the second week, then by the end of the year you will have £1,378 in your emergency fund. Without such a fund when an emergency occurs, such as your car needing new brakes, the only other option you have is to use a credit card to pay, which often involves incurring interest charges.

Ignoring estate-planning basics – this is not just about planning for your death, but also what will happen if you become too ill to work to support yourself. Ignoring this is crazy if you have dependents, as you are taking a huge risk by not having any contingencies or insurance in place for them to survive without your contribution.

In fact, it is totally irresponsible and the cost of not taking action can be catastrophic. I don't mean because you would be seriously ill or dead, but because you would've left those dependent on you in a financial pickle when they are not in a position to look after themselves financially and are having to deal with your illness or death.

If you have insurance or pension funds or Superannuation or 401K funds, then you can often lodge the names of your beneficiaries with your provider. I recently updated the beneficiaries of my main pension fund. It took just over fifteen minutes, and it only took that long because I had to look up my niece's and nephew's dates of birth and reset my password to login to the pension account!

Not getting serious about your retirement planning can also prove costly. The best time to start is as young as possible, but even if you are starting to save later on in life, it is at least better than not starting at all.

How much you need to have saved on retirement depends on how much you think you will need to live an acceptable standard of living.

If you need £30,000 to live on in retirement and you are expecting to retire at the age of 65, then you will need at least 20 years' worth of £30,000 to cover your retirement. You might want to cover 25 years; the decision is yours. Twenty years at £30,000 is a fund value of £600,000 when you retire. This is a simplistic view of retirement planning that will probably have many financial advisors cringing, but it gives you some focus. This should be the minimum you are aiming for.

This is not a full list of the things to consider but you will be able to see that there is a financial cost to procrastinating over dealing with your finances. You don't have to sort out any of these financial issues alone; you can use a professional such as an accountant or a financial advisor, seek help from a financial coach, or even discuss your money with your partner or family members.

It's Not A Crime

"Talking about money, are you crazy?" Yes, I can hear many of your thoughts as I write these words. Avoiding talk about money is one of those biases that is so tightly knit into our culture, it is hard to get over it.

Like many of you, my friends, and my coaching clients, I was raised in a family where it was impolite to talk about money. I used to think that this was a British thing, stiff upper lip and all that nonsense, but we are not the only ones not talking about money. In 2015, a study by Ally Bank in the USA found that 70% of Americans think that it is rude to talk about money.

We don't talk about how much we earn, how much we save, and how much debt we have, and we also don't talk about how much we pay in rent or mortgage repayments or how much our weekly shopping costs us. It appears that everything relating to money is often off limits.

Openly talking about money makes some people angry. Don't believe me? Then post a question about money and how much people are earning, saving, etc., on social media and see what responses you get. Some people really do think it's rude to talk about money, and yes, it is rude when it's not appropriate, but not talking about money at all is unhealthy.

My Law of Attraction mentor is Dr Joe Vitale, and if you've read the book or seen the film *The Secret*, then you will have heard of him. He has also written over thirty books, several of which have been number one bestsellers. I was once having a chat with another Law of Attraction coach that I know quite well, and she said that she didn't get on with Dr Joe and his teachings as she found him materialistic as he was always talking about the amazing cars and other things he had acquired. Why not though? He has manifested some amazing opportunities as well as his car collection and other items. He is not bragging as it's appropriate for his audience to know that he's able to manifest things.

Talking about money is not the same as bragging about your net worth, but who wants to brag anyway? It is, however, nice to share with your family and friends that you just bought a new car or upgraded to your dream home, and you might even share this good news on social media. That isn't bragging. People share everything about their lives on social media, from what restaurants they've dined in to which places they've holidayed at, so why is it sometimes seen as bragging to share news of material wealth? Well, it's not that you are bragging, it's that people think you are bragging. The problem here is with the people, for their mindset is telling them things like 'rich people are not very nice', as well as making them feel insecure that they might not be able to afford such items.

Talking about money is even more taboo than talking about sex, and I've read studies that have found that we are more likely to have sex with a new partner before talking about money with them. It's frightening to think that couples, those in long-term relationships and marriage, don't have frank discussions about money. According to a study by Fidelity Investments, 43% of Americans don't even know how much their spouse makes. If you can't be open and honest with your spouse about your money position, then who can you be open and honest with? Chances are you are also not being honest with yourself. This is the reason that fighting over money is a top reason for divorce.

Often, it's because we feel ashamed about not understanding financial matters that we don't talk to anyone else about them. This embarrassment conspires to keep us quiet. Getting to understand the basics of money management is key to facing this fear, and there isn't really that much that you need to know, it's just a matter of getting started.

If you're brave enough, why not start a conversation about money with someone close to you? Ask a question, solicit advice, tell your friend about this book. Start a conversation today.

Dampen The Flames

Do you feel like you have walked through fire just reading this chapter? If not, then I invite you to go back and read it again, and this time take some action. I don't say this to be flippant or arrogant, but if you acknowledge the fear in relation to your financial situation and make a plan to overcome that fear by addressing the practical elements of your finances that I've shared, then you will feel like you've walked through fire.

If your plan is to improve your financial situation, then you need to face the truth about your finances and start to take control. This is part mindset work, in becoming aware of the fear and not letting it control you, and part practical money management.

Reflections:

➢ Identify how fear is showing up for you in relation to your finances.

➢ What strategy is your fear allowing you to follow – are you doing nothing, abdicating responsibility or procrastinating? Create a mini-action plan for yourself to overcome these negative strategies.

➢ What practical action can you start to take to reduce the risk of procrastinating over your finances?

➢ Who do you need to start a conversation with about money? If you need to have a conversation and aren't yet ready to start the conversation, then journal the details so that you are sure that you understand fully, and then when you are ready, go ahead and have the conversation.

Affirmations:

➢ It is safe for me to invest in myself.
➢ My financial future is secure.
➢ I confidently talk to others about money matters.
➢ I have more than enough money for all my needs.

"You can do so little alone and so much together."

HELEN KELLER

9
Board of Directors

*Y*ou are the CEO of your life, but having a group to support and guide you can help you avoid a lot of headaches and costly mistakes. Such a group will nullify your weaknesses and allow you to tap into their areas of strength.

You will have no doubt heard the idea before that those with a wealth mindset actually select and utilise their board of directors. Inspired action is always the key.

Surround yourself with the people who get you, support you, help you take the leaps of faith and are ready to catch you if you stumble. Everyone needs their own board of directors. The right balance of relationships is important to have the right blend of people to provide the right support and perspective as opportunities and situations present themselves.

Who Do You Currently Listen To?

Back when I was an accountant, I often heard about the bloke in the pub who paid less tax and gave great financial advice. What used to scare me the most was when my client preferred to take the advice of a 'friend' or worse still, a friend of a friend. Taking second- and third-hand knowledge from people who are not experts is hardly the foundation for a solid wealth plan.

Who do you currently listen to? Whose advice around money, wealth and business are you taking?

Spouses and partners are a constant source of advice, and for the most part this advice is well meaning. Unfortunately, well-meaning does not always equate to the best advice. I like to think of them as a first port of call, a sounding board for ideas and concerns when you are in the initial stages of forming your idea or considering your problem.

Remember, when it comes to money though, they have their own relationship with money, their own limiting beliefs, and perhaps their own money goals. Listening to them may not be the best port of call when you're creating your wealth, unless you are able to have open and frank discussions about money and how they think about it.

Friends, they are wonderful human beings and you would not want to be without them, but they aren't necessarily the best advice-givers for helping you move forward. I have friends who support and encourage me, but I wouldn't ask for or take advice from them. To be fair to them, they would not offer advice either, and that works. You'll recognise who these friends are. Everyone has a role.

Wherever you are taking advice from, you need to spend some time examining if the situation is working for you. Do this on a regular basis, as people, with their unique experiences, change over time. Those close to you are grounded in the personal experiences that you share, and often don't want you to surge ahead and leave that sacred space or bond you've created. You cannot blame them for this.

It's just human nature to want to keep your circle intact, and you are part of that other person's circle of support and confidence. You can, of course, start to move away and push the boundaries. If the relationship is secure, then it's this moving in a higher direction, of creating more wealth and a more abundant lifestyle, that will push the boundaries of the bond you share. You know what though? Boundaries aren't set in stone. You can't halt your destiny just because others don't or can't move forward with you.

It's a very common money block to not want to leave your friends behind, if you were to become wealthy or successful in your business or career. You are responsible for yourself, and only yourself. Let me repeat this so that it sinks in: you are responsible for yourself and only yourself. Everyone else's thoughts and beliefs belong to them.

Next time you are writing in your journal, spend some time exploring who is currently in your board of directors, influencing your business success and affecting your ability to achieve the wealth that you desire.

Why would you want to follow someone else's rules and roadmap? I understand that it's difficult when you are married. I've never been married – though I got a little close on a couple of occasions – but I've never found anyone who I truly felt was following the same map as me, or if they were, they were clearly wanting to take a different route. It may be cynical, but shouldn't marriage or any long-term relationship be about taking a similar path? And you surely need to be on the same map, otherwise you are just co-habiting and that's not good for anyone in the longer term. You get one shot at this life, and while you might take many detours and learn lessons, you need to make sure that your life goes according to your rules.

This is why it's important to know your values and identify where you want to end up, which I talked about in the first couple of chapters. You can't live by your roadmap if you don't know what it looks like.

I often hear coaches, and indeed many people in business, stating that you should take the leap from employment to self-employment in whatever form that takes; that you aren't building *your* dream by working for someone else, you are just building   dream. It's the same with your personal life too. Yes, it takes courage and a loving relationship with yourself to have the strength to take the reins of your life and steer in the direction of your vision for the perfect future.

Be true to yourself. If you are not 100 percent sure who you are, then go back and read the first few chapters again and spend some time working on the things I talk about. If you are serious about creating the wealth and abundance that you desire, rather than just wishing you had it in your grasp, then you need to do whatever is necessary to discover who you truly are and what you want. Creating your dream team will help you do this.

Dream Team

Creating a dream team is something we all need to do. This team isn't just about those who help us push forward in our chosen profession but also those who help us free up our time to enable us to work in our zone of genius. This could mean having someone to do the ironing, cook meals, do the cleaning or walk the dogs.

When I last spoke to my friend Michelle, she had reached out to find a local person to take her dog for a long walk as her ill health was preventing her from doing so. She now swears that it's the best thing she has spent money on in a long time, freeing up her time to work on her business. The dog benefits too! Even now, with her health back to normal, she still uses the dog walker on a regular basis. The dog walker has become part of Michelle's dream team. Such support roles can be vital.

I've never really spent much time cleaning or ironing, and I hate both tasks if I have to do them for more than half an hour. They are called 'chores' for a reason. You can, however, always find people who are willing to do the tasks that you hate, so why not bring them into your team?

When should you bring them in? As soon as you possibly can or when you need them, and without getting into debt. Check out your budget and see what funds you can reallocate to start creating your team.

Do your sums. If you paid your cleaner £20 per hour but you earn £50 per hour, then it's a win-win situation. Even if you pay them £20 and, for now, only earn £20, then you still aren't losing out, as you are spending the time working on your business or working on achieving your money goals. I'm always amazed when I speak with women in my coaching business who have not done these sums and worked out what help they can bring in to support them move forward. The percentage of women who haven't done the sums is high. I've never calculated exact figures but it's a significant percentage, and I'm certain that they are representative of all the other women out there who are struggling to find the time and who need someone to delegate some tasks to.

Getting help that you need works wonders for improving your mindset, as it does feel abundant to have people helping you in this way. When you feel more abundant living a business-class or first-class lifestyle, then you start to attract more wealth and abundance. The Law of Attraction comes into play.

This is all about delegation, but you must have people around you that you can give these tasks to.

The same applies to help in your business. I know some fantastic virtual assistants and business admin support people who absolutely love what they do and are efficient at it. In fact, I've been one of those support people with my accountancy practice in the past. I know I've certainly helped many clients to grow their businesses as they've not had to worry about their financials – they could depend on me to provide the analysis they needed, when they needed it.

In fact, if you have good business support, they often gauge what you need well before you know it yourself, as they're working in their zone of genius and know what the options are.

Yes, you can have employees. Some business models require this. I do have a tainted view on having employees and would never want full-time employees again, but my model of working doesn't strictly require me to have them. However, I have clients and friends who have a large team of employees as their businesses are structured in the traditional model for growth.

If that's how you work, you need to ensure you create your dream team for delegating tasks within this workforce. There are many good books out there that can help you with this. Creating an excellent team of employees is not my zone of genius – plus, my views on this subject are too tainted for me to give any constructive advice – but you need to figure out a way that works for you and find the help that enables you to do so, whether that's from coaches or self-help books.

It's not just your household and employee team that you can lean on for support to free up your time. There are many other areas where you can outsource tasks. Create a list of who you would like to have on your team, keep adding to the list when you find a new task that you could outsource, and then when your budget permits, you can take action, free your time and concentrate on working towards your financial freedom.

The Professionals

When you are considering who should be part of your dream team, remember to include the finance and business professionals. Ask any successful business owner and they'll confirm that they have a team of coaches and mentors. Different coaches and mentors will come into your life as you grow and develop your business and streams of income.

Mentors and coaches serve as role models you can follow and emulate. You can get to know a lot about someone and what they have to offer by following them on social media. Remember though that you are only seeing what they allow you to see, and the information they share is sometimes well-constructed to portray themselves in a certain way.

A coach is someone who you generally work with for a short period of time and on a particular skill set or problem area that you are facing. The support that they give you is often quite formal and structured as they help you develop in their areas of expertise. They will become your partner in working stuff out. 'Stuff', of course, is a generic term that I like to use, but you can replace it with words such as marketing planning, business planning, confidence building, and so on. In fact, the list can go on and on, as you can be coached in almost anything.

A mentor, on the other hand, is someone who's there to play devil's advocate, to be directive in telling you which way to do something. Often the relationship with a mentor, while deep rooted, is more informal and flexible than the arrangements you have with a coach. Some of your mentors might be people within your circle, so you can tap into their expertise and guidance for free. If this is the case, you should always be mindful that their expertise does have a value and that mentors, being successful people, are often short on time. They can help you though with specific challenges; just be ready to listen to them, make notes and be prepared to go away and implement their suggestions on your own. They won't be holding your hand like a coach might. They will help you to be reactive to situations rather than acquiring new skills.

Mentors are successful in their field, and can share their wisdom to provide insight into their zone of genius and passion. Mentors aren't cheap to hire. Not because they are greedy, although some of course may be, but because they can earn high amounts doing what they do best. They certainly will only be able to mentor a few people at once, and most of the mentoring work will be conducted on a one-to-one basis, with any coaching elements being delivered in a group environment.

Sometimes the only way you will be able to afford a mentor, at least in the beginning of your journey to wealth, is by attending any events they may hold. Any chance you get to hang out in their presence will be valuable.

Back in the day when I had my accountancy practice, I used to attend workshops and other events held by a group of guys in my profession who were, in my opinion, at the cutting edge of how the profession was developing – not from a technical point of view, but in terms of how accountants were evolving and providing more beneficial services to their clients. I attended everything they hosted over a course of twelve to eighteen months. They had a nickname for people like me: 'seminar junkie'. I was okay with that, since I was learning not only by picking up the skills that were being taught on the course, but also by spending time talking with them.

Sometimes, you can learn as much at lunchtime by sitting next to the right person, as you can from a whole day's seminar. I wasn't the average seminar junkie though. This was my form of stalking them, in a legal way, to gain the knowledge and expertise that is sometimes hard to teach in a structured manner. They were, in fact, my mentors at this time.

Did it pay off? Yes, it did, as my accountancy practice grew at a considerable rate, my income trebled, and I was able to explore other areas where I eventually found my true calling. Through my connection with these fabulous mentors, I also got to travel to the United States and Australia, which aren't the typical business trips for a UK based Chartered Accountant.

I did eventually one day decide to take the plunge and pay the £1,500 daily fee for a one-to-one mentoring session. It would be unfair to them to say that I was disappointed, but I didn't really learn much on that day. It was my way of giving back to them for all the help and support that they had given me. Besides, it also helped me move on to the next phase of my business journey, where I needed to find new mentors. I didn't know that at the time though, but that's where reflection helps.

Accountants / professional advisors. While professional advice is a good thing, you should always know enough about your finances to know what questions to ask. Not all professionals are created equal when it comes to technical ability, let alone in their ability to offer professional advice.

I think I can criticise the profession as I've been there myself, as a Chartered Accountant and Independent Financial Advisor here in the UK. Accountants are trained to put the numbers together in accordance with Company Law and Tax Legislation and to interpret the figures, but that's about it. It's a very narrow view.

Often, they don't really run their accountancy practice as a real business and may lack the necessary level of experience or technical knowledge, so are they the best people to go to for advice on creating wealth and growing your business? There are some who are bloody fantastic. When choosing your professional advisors, you need to make your decision on the recommendation of others along with your own gut feelings.

Financial advisors, at a basic level, are trained to sell you financial products. Their exams are about understanding what their products do and who they are useful for. For many, it's a narrow view, so they are interested in selling you the 'product' – meaning, any advice they give will be linked to closing the sale.

I don't mean to be cynical here, but I know many women who have been in 'awe' of their financial advisor and have taken everything they say as 100 percent truth, even when it hasn't necessarily been in their best interest. You do need to take responsibility for your money plan and know where you are heading. If you can articulate this to your financial advisors, then they can at least help you achieve those goals or point you in the right direction.

If you find an advisor who can help, then hang on to them, pay them their worth and nurture that relationship.

Your Soul Family

"A lot of people have gone further than they could because someone else thought they could."

- Zig Ziglar

Your soul family, or your 'tribe', are rare finds and should become treasured possessions. You need to be on the lookout for them, even search for them if you need to. I've used the Law of Attraction to bring people into my life – some of them served their purpose and left, others hung around and became great friends, but one or two of them have developed into being part of my inner tribe.

When someone is the right fit for this tribe, they will love you unconditionally without any judgement. You will feel a strong sense of connection and be extremely comfortable in their presence.

Sometimes this happens almost immediately, as if you have known each other all your lives, and others may require time for the connection to be truly made. It doesn't matter how quickly the connection is formed, what matters more is *how* it is formed, as this is often a necessary part of your combined journey.

The people who become part of your tribe might already be in your life. They can be your family, friends or people who you meet through networking groups. The problem with finding such people in networking groups is the difficulty in finding a group that connects with your ethos and that brings together like-minded people to work together.

Not all networking groups are created equal; some are just interested in passing business and the proverbial business card. I have, in fact, given up having business cards. Anyone who just wants to collect my business card is not someone who wants to develop a relationship with me.

When you find a great networking group, you will be able to meet people who individually or collectively stretch your thinking and challenge your assumptions. I spend half a day, once a month, attending a group of like-minded women a couple of towns away. Many of the women haven't been in business as long as I have, most aren't at the same earning capacity as me, but that doesn't matter, because as a collective we are like-minded and able to support each other. From this group I have formed a number of close business relationships with women who are becoming members of my tribe.

Forming strategic relationships – that is, those relationships that are mutually beneficial to all the parties concerned – will give you the opportunity to learn, grow, advance in your business and bring greater value. These relationships, while formed in the business arena, can run as long and as deep as personal ones.

It isn't just in-person connections that are important. Modern technology and the popularity of social media and networking sites such as Facebook and LinkedIn can provide connections much further afield, even across oceans and on the other side of the world. You can have conversations over Skype, Zoom and the many other platforms available. Technology has made the world small. This can be to your advantage.

There are many inspirational women and businesswomen on social media. You just need to find those women that move something in you. You can connect with them and their business, read about what they teach, watch their videos and connect with their passion. This doesn't always lead to them becoming part of your 'tribe', but they can still be a significant influence on the way you think and act and boost your ability to propel your business forward.

Attracting such people into your life does take some effort and thought, just as with pretty much everything else that we do with purpose. A key element is to learn to love yourself. Remember, like attracts like. The love that we are able to give and receive in our relationships is only as powerful as the love that we have for ourselves. Of course, some of your tribe may come to you so that you can learn to love yourself more.

This was certainly true with my dear friend Heather. She came into my life at a time when I had healed myself as much as I could with outside influence and guidance. I was honestly astonished that someone could value my opinion and accept me for who I was to the extent that she did, which in turn helped me on the road to loving myself.

Life Is An Echo

On a final note, I'd like to bring in another universal law which is important to grasp when creating your wealthy life, and that is the Law of Reciprocity. According to Wikipedia, *"reciprocity is a social form of responding to a positive action with another positive action."* My Nan would have said this means that you reap what your sow.

In basic terms, this means that you cannot gain something without giving something of equivalent value such as time, money or talent.

This is important to remember when you're putting together your soul tribe or your board of directors. It is not just about finding people who can help you and enrich your life, but also who you can help.

Is there an element of fair exchange with each member of your team? It's a tough question to ask ourselves as we often like to think we are giving back and that we are predisposed to responding to positivity with positivity, to kindness with kindness.

As children, many of us were told not to always take as that wasn't very nice, but to instead be generous and make sure we shared. As with a lot of things that we are taught as children, this is perfectly true, but for some of us these stories have been propelled out of proportion.

So, for us to remain in equilibrium and have a sense of fair exchange, we need to give as well as take. When we are considering putting together our board of directors, this is worth careful consideration.

While explaining this concept to Lisa in one of our coaching sessions, she said, "You mean the whole board needs to be on a see-saw, in balance with me sitting in the middle." I love this analogy as it's a great visual representation of what you are trying to create.

You'll offer some people on your board your support in return, some you will pay for their input, and some will receive a mix of support and payment, but however it is established make sure you are in equilibrium. You are giving and receiving and creating a harmonious setting in which you can thrive, while helping others in their journey. Wow, it does not get much better than that.

Who Is On Your Board?

Some careful planning is needed when putting together your personal and business board of directors.

Are the people you are currently listening to for money advice equipped to do so impartially and for your best interest? It's a tough call at times, but putting some on the subs bench can make a world of difference to your ability to move forward.

Give yourself the time to plan who you want on your dream team. When I had a traditional business with employees, someone once told me that it was best to hire slow and sack fast. While you may not be in the corporate world, there is still probably an important lesson in there, especially the hire slow part – make sure you are bringing in the types of people (with the services they offer) that are the most valuable to you

Remember that professional advisors, while sometimes expensive, can be worth their weight in gold. Choose carefully though and ensure that they understand what you are trying to achieve.

Create alliances that work for you and ensure you become part of someone else's team.

Reflections:

> Examine the advice you last received and if it helped or hindered you, no matter how well intentioned it had been.

> Are those close to you more or less wealthy than you? Examine how this affects your relationships.

> Create a list of positions that you would like to add to your board, so that you know who to be on the lookout for. Put the list in order of preference once you have the funds available to bring them on board.

> Examine if your money beliefs and aspirations in the future are in alignment with the professional advisors that you have on board. If they are not in alignment, plan to find new advisors.

> Examine your prime relationships and determine if they are in equilibrium. Is there a sense of fair exchange? If not, what can you do to bring these relationships into equilibrium?

Affirmations:

- ➢ It is safe for me to ask for help.
- ➢ I am unaffected by the opinions of others.
- ➢ I am able to clearly communicate my expectations to others.
- ➢ I encourage my friends to follow their dreams just as they encourage me to fulfill mine.

"Action is the foundational key to all success."

PABLO PICASSO

10
Roadmap to Financial Freedom

*T*he way to achieve your financial freedom is to live within your means and dream big and take inspired action, and not be confined by the glass walls and ceilings that can be easily created around us.

Of course, it all depends on what you consider to be financial freedom. It's more than something that can be measured in monetary terms, although numbers play an important role. It's about how it makes you feel, how it allows you to live your life.

Reading these words I can feel the excitement of what financial freedom means to me, as well as see the movie in my mind of what this looks like. These feelings and visualisation are what will keep you motivated and act as a reminder to your mind, so it can spot opportunities to create the wealth you desire. With this mindset, you can push the boundaries of your comfort zone. Scary but exhilarating at the same time, like being on those fast rides at the fun fair without the need to go to the fair.

When creating your roadmap to financial freedom, you must first decide how much money you need to live the life you desire.

Embrace The Change

For most of us, pursuing change is hard as our minds are wired to be on repeat, carrying out the same tasks and activities. "If you always do what you've always done, you'll always get what you've always got." This is true. You don't create wealth by doing what you've always done. Even when you are already wealthy, you will be constantly evaluating your income streams and your desired outcome, preparing to make the necessary changes to keep you on course.

Yet, everything that we have in our life right now, including all the good stuff that has appeared along the way, is the result of change. This change has been happening in small unnoticeable ways, with tweaks to how we operate being made here and there over time, as we encounter new experiences and gain new knowledge.

Change happens to us all; there is no point trying to avoid it. Change for change's sake will often not produce your ideal outcome, but when it is part of your journey towards financial freedom then it's easier to embrace. Notice that I said easier, not easy. Change can be good for us if we embrace it as a tool to get us to our destination. It's when we make a change, don't get more favourable results, and then don't revert to the original plan that things can start to go a little astray. A hard lesson I've learned from many entrepreneurial journeys. It took me several misadventures to discover this, all worthwhile lessons nonetheless.

Change is to do with your mental attitude and your beliefs. It may scare you, but the more you work on your vision, the easier it becomes to take the necessary steps. When you know where you are heading, you'll know in your gut as your unconscious tells you what to do and where to go. Opportunities will feel right to you, and you will easily be able to dismiss those that don't feel right and won't get you the outcome that you desire.

It's about gaining energetic momentum. You start by taking action. My Law of Attraction mentor, Dr Joe Vitale, says that the Universe loves speed. In other words, strike while the iron is hot. I used to worry about this, as I didn't always have time to work on ideas as they came to me, especially as ideas and opportunities often come careening like buses – you can wait for a long time for one and then several turn up at the same time. Dr Joe explained to me that all I needed to do was start the action process with each new idea, make notes to get the idea out of my head and on to paper, and work out some of the details. Sometimes I needed to have others take action first, so I could set them to work while I went about finishing off more pressing matters. Sometimes, just organising my thoughts on paper was all the action I needed to take, especially in the initial stages.

With any change that you take, you must be willing to fail. Put yourself out there and take the chance, and the Universe will reward you for taking this action. Being willing and planning for failure are two separate things and have a different impact on your mindset. With each new venture, whether it be a new training programme, a coaching package or a new book, I plan to succeed but unless I am willing to accept that it is possible that the idea may fail, I could be stuck with the ideas still in my notebook. A key point to remember is that you must fail fast. Another lesson I learned the hard way, as my 'failures' all seemed to be slow agonising deaths. When things seem wrong to you, there is a good chance that they are indeed wrong and it's time to plan a swift exit.

Having said all of this, it doesn't mean that you should take foolish risks. Do as I say, not as I have done!

Inspired action is about turning inwards and getting the green light to go ahead. Feeling the internal nudge to do something that feels right for you and the direction you are heading in.

Every change you make starts in the mind, at the instant when you make the decision to do something different. You need to make that decision as soon as possible so that you can become wealthy.

Choose How To Work

We need to work; money won't fall from the sky. There are of course different ways we can earn our money.

You can have **earned income**, the kind of money you get from your job. Certainly, when you first start the journey to creating a business, you might find it useful to keep a hold of your job. I get it, I did it, I have friends who have done it. My advice to anyone in this position is that you won't get serious about making your money from a business until you have ditched the job. The key is to put together your products or services, just one or two basic components, trial them, tweak them if necessary, and then get to the position where you can make the leap to working full-time in your business as soon as possible. Don't let your comfort zone, of having the security of a wage each month, keep you away from leading a wealthy life.

Money from something you sell is a **profit**. Well, it is a profit if you sell it for more than it costs! The main principle that you need to learn before going in business. It's a simple but important formula, income less costs equals profit. Profit is the name of the game. Income is a great indicator for how your business is progressing and helps you understand your business while providing vital information to help with decision making, but it is profit that trumps income. If you don't have profits, then you are not creating wealth. In fact, you are doing the opposite.

If having a business is new to you and you don't have huge amounts to invest, then you have a few options. Try turning a hobby or interest into a business, as you won't be as overwhelmed with the process of creating a business when you are doing something that you are already experienced in. Network marketing companies are also a good starting point. I know many women who started out in network marketing, and they either made it to the top or used the company to tap into awesome business and personal development guidance. It's usually under £200 to join, making it a no-brainer decision.

Let's be clear. Running your own business is not for the faint hearted as it can entail long hours, especially in the beginning, and it is often not as much fun as you expect it to be when you start out – or was that just me?

If you have your own business and you're already making good money, then you know just having a business doesn't give you the wealth you require. There is a little more to it than just setting up a business for yourself. To start, you need to be in business doing something that you really enjoy, so that you look forward to working and growing your business.

I meet many women who are trying to branch out into self-employment. Starting a business while you work at your job allows you to test the waters while still retaining the security of receiving money every month. The best time to break free of the shackles of your job depends on each person, but it needs to be just as you become confident in your business. Waiting until your income matches your salary will keep you tied in your job far longer than necessary.

A tip here is to save a fund for your first year of going it alone, as that will help take the stress out of losing your salary. It's a comfort blanket that will pay your expenses for five to six months if things don't go according to plan in the beginning. This fund is from savings from your after-tax earnings in your side-hustle.

Do not add the money you make from your business venture to your salary, or you'll soon become accustomed to living off the newer higher income levels. If you have debt, then instead of creating a savings fund you should concentrate on eliminating your debt as soon as possible. Take away this burden and you'll find it easier to cut ties with employment.

Learning business skills and the allure of passive income, there is no wonder that multi-level marketing companies are so popular. They do provide an excellent way for people to branch out into becoming a business owner. Often the problem is that people join such companies expecting to replace salaries within three months or so. It could take years, just like with any business. If it's going to take you nine years to replace your salary so that you have the same level of income, but that level of income isn't depending on you working forty hours per week, won't this be a good decision to make?

I particularly like the good MLM companies as they give you the business training you need, as well as the personal development training. Like with all choices in life, you need to do your homework, do your due diligence, pick a reputable company that sells a product that you can feel excited about.

A business buddy of mine recently wanted to take a couple of months off work to look after her sick mother. Her siblings didn't have passive income and could only take limited time off work, but as she had passive income from her MLM business that she had been on for the last three years, she could take a couple of months off and still get paid. This is the power of passive income; it gives you freedom and flexibility, and that's what financial freedom is for most of us. There are other avenues that you can take to create passive income streams such as creating online courses. Whatever option you decide, you need to start to take action.

Entrepreneurial Journey

I recently read a magazine article which stated that millionaires typically have seven streams of income, and certainly the millionaires that I know have several streams of income. Diversifying your portfolio and not relying on just one source of income is common sense. This is something you need to bear in mind as you develop your plans for your business, remembering the definition of a business owner.

This doesn't mean you need to plan to develop seven businesses. That's a sure-fire way to be on a fast track to burn out. For some, these different streams will be different types of core products within the same business, but there can also be income streams outside of operating your business.

Most people rarely become wealthy by working for others and it is therefore likely that you will not become wealthy by just having a 'job'. If you follow the crowd, then you will achieve the same as they do. If you want the same results that's fine, but if you truly want to live a wealthy lifestyle, then you will need to make some changes.

The book *Rich Dad, Poor Dad* has gained something of a cult following, and there is a reason for it. This book had a big revelation for me. I had known that being an employee was not going to lead to wealth, and I knew being a business owner was the way forward, yet with my accountancy practice, I had fallen into the trap like so many owners of small businesses. Such ventures are not a business at all.

Wow, I had spent nearly ten years working on building a practice that, while it had some value, was not worth the blood, sweat and tears it took controlling cash flow, dealing with clients, managing employees and all the other headaches that come with having a traditional business.

I had created a job for myself, with all the additional headaches that you do not generally have as an employee. I no longer had just my mortgage payments to worry about but also the mortgages of thirteen other families. This was not the way to achieve financial freedom.

If you have a business that is entirely dependent on your time, then, like me, you are self-employed but not a business owner. For me this was like being punched in the stomach. Just take a moment to think about this – what will happen if you stop working?

Will your income stop?

If you have an employee, what happens to their income in the long term? Will they be able to pay their mortgage?

Will you be able to pay yours?

To be a true business owner, you need to enter the realm of entrepreneurs. They are the people who design systems, which comprise processes and sometimes people, to generate a profit. It's about creating a business that can earn profit even if you are not working. This gives you freedom. Freedom to start living the life you want to, and freedom to create further income streams.

But won't I need to work hard for my money? Did that thought go through your head? It did keep creeping into my mind as I worked on building my new business. It kept pulling me back towards being self-employed, but as you work on changing your money story and eliminating limiting beliefs, you will stop having such thoughts and be able to build your business faster.

The quickest way is to own your own business. Start with becoming self-employed and then you can work on moving into being an entrepreneur. You have skills already; you are employed for those skills now if you have a job. If you are unsure what you'd like to do for a business, then start off by making a list of all the things you can do well and that people would be willing to pay you money for. You might be surprised at what other people want to outsource to someone else as they do not like doing the task themselves or they don't have the time. You might clean their house, do their ironing, prepare and schedule their social media posts, chase their customers for money owed, bookkeeping, or type manuscripts. The list is endless.

You need to think smart before becoming self-employed – narrow down your list to those that you will be able to turn into a passive or semi-passive income stream. You don't need to know this straight away but if you can see this future income stream for any skill that you have, then you should choose to pursue this venture.

Source of Your Cash

If you already have some spare cash, then you will be able to earn **interest income** as a result of lending the money to someone, putting it in the bank or lending it to the government in the form of Bonds or Treasury Bills.

An equally passive source of income is **dividend income**, which you receive if the company you invest in performs well, creates a profit and then decides to distribute some of that wealth to its shareholders. Knowing which stocks and shares to invest in is a separate book topic, but it is a source of income that you should be aware of.

Then there is **rental income** which is the income you get as a result of renting out an asset. For most people who are generating rental income, this asset is a property. You do however require capital to invest in property, which is a downside when you don't have much. You might be able to acquire a mortgage to buy the property, but this comes with inherent risks as the mortgage needs repaying even if you don't have any tenants in the property.

It's typically easier to invest in savings accounts or companies to earn interest or dividends than it is to invest in property, although there are property investment funds that can help you utilise this asset category.

You should also consider the liquidity of your investments, that is, how quickly you can gain access to your cash if you need to. If it is difficult to get hold of your cash in the investment, such as having to sell a property, then this could impact any future events.

It's advisable to have a balanced portfolio. Learning more about this topic or talking to a financial advisor will help you avoid the pitfalls. Remember, even if you use the services of a financial advisor, you need to understand what is happening to your money. It is your responsibility and only yours.

Royalty income is the money that you get as a result of letting someone use your products or processes. They do all the hard work, make all the revenues, and then you get a small percentage of what they earn. A franchise is a great example of this. If you buy into a franchise such as McDonald's (assuming you can afford the capital outlay), you'll pay a percentage to McDonald's to be able to use their name and systems.

The challenge here is to create something that is unique and that you can make repeatable.

The final source of income is called **capital gains**. This is the income you receive as a result of an increase in the value of an asset that you own. For example, if you buy shares for £100 and then sell them for £120, you have made £20 in capital gains. Again, this is a form of income that requires you to have some cash to invest in the first place, but it is worth considering for the future, for when you can invest.

So, go on, choose your streams. As you read through the types of income streams that are possible, remember that the first stage is to start a business. Start with one thing, one business, one product, become an expert in your niche, and then make sure that the business can run without your constant input.

The biggest risk to your financial life is being dependent on only one income stream where you are actively involved full-time.

Follow The Breadcrumbs

Panic and overwhelm are common feelings when faced with leaving the security of a job. I see it all the time with women who are looking to expand their horizons and becoming financially independent. These feelings never completely leave you until you have developed your product or service and have successfully launched it to the marketplace.

Remember, you choose your mindset. If you worry and panic, you become the victim and end up operating in scarcity mode. Or you can look at the story differently, as new opportunities, which will take you further towards financial freedom. This is choosing the abundance mindset. Sitting on the fence doesn't form part of a successful strategy here. Everyone needs to start somewhere; you need to decide if you are going to start the process or sit on the fence. It's a choice. It's your choice.

Once you have made your choice, you will have started the process of inspired action. Ideas will come to you, little nudges of divine inspiration, and the more steps you take, the more nudges the Universe will give you. It's like rolling a snowball down a hill, it will soon pick up more snow and more speed as it goes further along its chosen path. The small actions you take will add to this snowball effect, giving you more and more power to create the wealthy life that you have chosen.

New things sometimes cannot happen until you let go of the old and move on. While I loved working part-time as a finance director and found the job interesting, it was for the most part holding me back from exploring my true passion. Having previously handed in my notice to only return to the position two weeks after leaving, I found myself being tempted by the new managing director of the exciting times ahead and that perhaps I should work more hours. I wasn't swayed as my purpose was becoming clearer to me, but I wasn't ready to leave again either. I was sitting on the fence, just for a short while, but I continued to work on developing my own income streams. The Universe took the situation in hand, and after a blazing argument with the owner of the business, which came out of the blue, all bridges were well and truly burnt and I had no choice but to go it alone, ready or not.

It wasn't a smooth transition to being fully self-employed again. I became ill with my repetitive ear infections. It was fortunate that I had my savings fund for supporting this transition period. A wise lady helped me to understand that while the anger around the situation that led to my leaving was needed to get me to leave and never go back, it had also left me with emotions that needed to be worked through. This anger that I had was manifesting itself in my body by giving me repeated ear infections. Now they say that things happen for a reason. Well, this time served to remind me of the spiritual influence and work that I had previously resisted because it didn't conform to my years of training of being analytical and having clearly defined systems.

It was time to move to new thinking. Default thinking will give you default results. New thinking, along with the inspired action you take, will give you the desired change you need to head towards your more abundant lifestyle. You just need to follow the breadcrumbs.

Creating Your Map

Each of us will take a different journey to financial freedom, as we are starting from a unique position and have our own ideal end location in mind. It therefore makes sense that our roadmaps will not look the same.

You can choose to follow one of the many experts out there in social media land who have a 'proven' blueprint to financial success. It might seem tempting to follow in their footsteps because let's face it, we would all love to know what the shortcuts are. I do recommend this course of action.

My words of warning though, are to find someone who has a blueprint that will help you get from where you are now to where you want to be. You need to find a near match and be prepared for their roadmap to only take you on part of your journey. Watch out for the fork in the road, where you need to jump onto a different map to get you where you are headed.

Armed with the basics I've mentioned in this chapter, you now have what you need to start creating your own roadmap.

Reflections:

- ➤ What action are you willing to take right now to start to change your wealth?
- ➤ If you knew that you could not fail, what would you do to generate the level of wealth that you desire?
- ➤ Take the time to journal your ideas for earning more wealth.
- ➤ What are the current sources of your income? Do you need to give any sources up, now or in the future, to enable you to follow a wealthier path?
- ➤ What skills and resources do you need to ensure that you work your way to the next stage of your map to financial freedom?

Affirmations:

- ➤ Saving money is natural to me.
- ➤ Money comes to me easily and frequently.
- ➤ It is safe for me to become wealthy.
- ➤ I am on the road to financial freedom.

Resources

Sacred Money Archetypes®

To access the details of your money personality profile, you can take the quiz here:

www.jooutram.com/sacred-money-archetypes-quiz

Demartini – Value Determination Process

https://drdemartini.com/values

MOT your finances – Checklist

➢ Is your financial paperwork organised? Make sure it's in date order for each category of expenditure.

➢ Are your bill payments up to date? If not, create a list of outstanding bills.

➢ Review your monthly and quarterly bills and make sure you are being charged correctly, and where possible, look for alternative suppliers who are cheaper.

➢ Review your bank statements, credit card statements and PayPal account to ensure you are not being charged for items you no longer need, such as subscriptions or membership fees.

➢ Review your budget and spending habits to determine the areas you can improve. If you don't have a budget, then make time to prepare one.

➢ Create a plan to get rid of your debt once and for all. If you already have a plan in place, then make sure to review it on a regular basis and make any necessary revisions.

➢ Check out your credit rating and credit file, if you have not done so in the last three months. Make sure that your credit file does not contain any incorrect information. Sign up to a free credit checking service, if not currently subscribed.

➢ If your credit rating is in good standing and you have credit card debt, then consider transferring your balances to cards with zero interest. Watch out for any transfer fees and other terms before making any transfer.

➢ Review your savings plan. Are your savings in line with your goals? Is your emergency fund at an appropriate level (around three to six months' worth of expenses)? If you have credit card debt, plan to get this fund to £300 – £1,000 until you clear your debt.

➢ Check your investment and pension accounts and see if any rebalancing is needed, or if you can afford to pay in more each month.

Acknowledgments

*F*irstly, my appreciation goes to my parents, for teaching me great lessons about money, even if I didn't interpret them correctly until recently! More importantly, for taking me in and being there when I needed you the most and for giving me the space to heal my relationship with money without judging me.

Thank you to Lara Young for her guidance and support as I trained with her at The Mindset Coach Academy, to take my mindset coaching to the next level.

To my wonderful friends, including Heather Harris and Di Barnett, who help me to feel like my contribution to the world can be inspirational to others.

My gratitude also goes to my mastermind ladies, Claire Cahill, Andrea Gillard and Deborah Hoult, who continue to support me to achieve my goals, who allow me to run my ideas past them, and who remind me of what I am capable of.

About The Author

*J*o is a Chartered Accountant, Independent Financial Advisor and Business Owner. She has also authored several journals and books about finances, taxes and abundance (including being a co-author with Law of Attraction Guru, Joe Vitale, *The Abundance Factor*).

Her journey to financial success hasn't always been smooth – despite her two decades in the financial industry. Why? Well, like many smart women in business, she didn't grasp the importance of adopting a positive money mindset. So despite her extensive financial industry experience, she found herself with a business on the verge of financial collapse in 2009.

Thankfully, this pivotal time led her to discover the Law of Attraction – the key to her biggest financial breakthrough yet – and she has never looked back.

Equipped with a new money story and an abundance strategy that helped her avoid bankruptcy, become debt-free and turn her finances around forever, Jo knew she'd discovered her real vocation.

So in 2015, she founded her Financial Fitness Instructor business and has since been sharing her secrets to financial success and abundance through one-to-one coaching, an online VIP Financial Fitness Club and her books and programmes. In 2019 she became a Certified Mindset Coach and Sacred Money Archetypes® Coach.

Her mission? To support women in business from all over the world to become financially fit, create a healthy money mindset and blitz those limiting beliefs that have held them back for too long.

Find out more about Jo and how she can support your financial success journey via her website: jooutram.com

Ways to Work With Jo

Financial Fitness – Get Smart About Your Money

Stuck in a financial rut?

Unable to organise your money?

Confused about where your hard-earned cash disappears to each month?

In this book, Financial Fitness, Jo takes you through a practical process of help you organise your financial affairs and understand your current position, to create a debt elimination plan, ensure you are saving appropriately and helps you develop an action plan to increase your overall level of financial fitness.

Become A Money Magnet

Imagine if you could get your money organised in a way that takes the emotion out of the equation. Wouldn't it be great if you had a formula to follow so you could make sure you had all your bases covered?

This online eCourse and coaching program is for female business owners to create the money mindset needed for a life of financial success and the eradication of money-related stress, following Jo's 5 keys to abundance formula.

To find out more, go to https://bit.ly/5bamm

9 780645 067354